D0535155

How's the **Squid?**

"What'll it be, handsome?"

How's the Squid?

A Book of Food Cartoons

by Jack Ziegler

Harry N. Abrams, Inc., Publishers

A C K N O W L E D G M E N T S

Thanks to Lee Lorenz, William Shawn, Bob Mankoff, David Remnick, Harvey Kurtzman, Michelle Urry, Doug Kenney, Brian McConnaichie, Christopher Sweet, Sigi Nacson, Jane Cavolina, and the maniacs at the Cartoon Bank.

Project Manager: Christopher Sweet
Editor: Sigi Nacson
Series Designer: Robert McKee
Designer: Miko McGinty and Maki Takenouchi
Production Manager: Kaija Markoe

Library of Congress Cataloging-in-Publication Data

Ziegler, Jack.
How's the squid? : a book of food cartoons / by Jack Ziegler.
p. cm.
Includes bibliographical references and index.
ISBN 0-8109-5602-0 (hardcover)
1. Food--Caricatures and cartoons.
2. American wit and humor, Pictorial. I. Title.

NC1429.Z47A4 2004
741.5'973--dc22

2004003433

Published in 2004 by Harry N. Abrams, Incorporated, New York.

Printed and bound in China

10 9 8 7 6 5 4 3 2 1

Harry N. Abrams, Inc.
100 Fifth Avenue
New York, N.Y. 10011
www.abramsbooks.com

LA MARTINIÈRE GROUPE

*"Today the secret ingredients for Mom's Apple Pie
were sold to the Japanese for sixty-eight million dollars."*

To Kelli, who taught me how to use a knife and fork.

"We suburb, son; therefore, we grill."

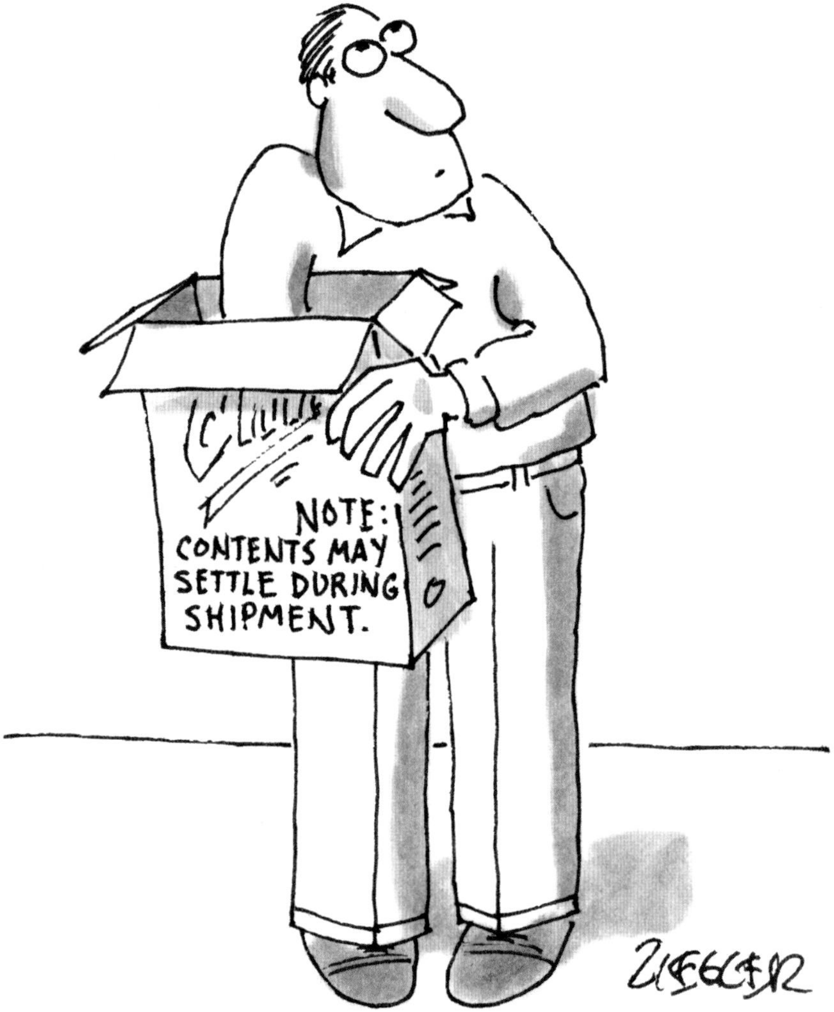
NOTE:
CONTENTS MAY
SETTLE DURING
SHIPMENT.
ZIEGLER

Introduction

Typically I like to start my day with a bowl of Cheerios that has a banana sliced into it. The banana should be at that delicate stage when it has still got a bit of green left on the skin, but has not yet begun to freckle. This is peak-flavor time and can last as long as a week in winter, but only two days, if you're lucky, in summer. Some time ago a bunch of green bananas came into my possession and I set them aside, waiting for them to reach their peak.

It never came. Two weeks later they were still green and hard as desert rocks. I cut into one and an unpleasant milky fluid leached out. I cringed in horror and then tossed the whole lot into the trash.

While waiting for bananas to ripen, it's important to have a standby cereal. Mine used to be Raisin Bran. When purchasing this tasty and bowel-friendly treat, it's important to note the expiration date on the package. At least a year in the future is good. Anything less and you've made a deal with the devil. I once bought a box without scanning the expiration and when I opened it and poured some into a bowl, I noticed a slight movement prior to adding milk. Upon inspection, wriggling larvae were clearly visible and then a small moth began to struggle over the lip of the bowl.

That was three years ago and I still can't go near the stuff, no matter how fresh it claims to be.

And raisins and bananas do not stand alone in their fruity cloak of supposed innocence. Seafood is another crapshoot. They say that if fish smells like fish, it's already gone by. What's *that* all about? If meat, on the other hand, still smells like meat, go for it.

How about vegetables? If celery is soft and draping off the side of the plate, dump it. When there's vegetation growing out of the sack of potatoes in your pantry, cast it aside. And if the can of tomato soup on the shelf above the potatoes is ballooning, that's not a good sign, either.

Milk should be white and free of lumps. Keep butter refrigerated, lest it turn instantly rancid. When chocolate develops a bloom, beware. Cheese should look like cheese, not the dusty linoleum floor of your bathroom.

When a friend gifts you with a box of crackers and some homemade dip as a special Yuletide treat, try to get to it before Valentine's Day. Don't leave that doggie bag from your favorite French restaurant sitting in the back seat of your car over a humid August weekend.

And remember that piece of driftwood that was lying out on the beach for several days? Why did you scrape the mussels off of it and then expect to do your friends a favor by treating their taste buds to your Mama's old-world recipe for seafood marinara? Why, why, why? Once they were released from the hospital, they never spoke to you again.

Well, okay, they never spoke to *me* again. I suppose I can't blame them. But gee, I had the best intentions in the world. I'm sure they know that. But still, a little forgiveness would be nice someday.

Because, after all, every damn last one of them knows full well that I hate the stigma that goes with that most humiliating of urban experiences—dining alone.

—*Jack Ziegler, Las Vegas, 2004*

Sunrise on Mount Hibachi

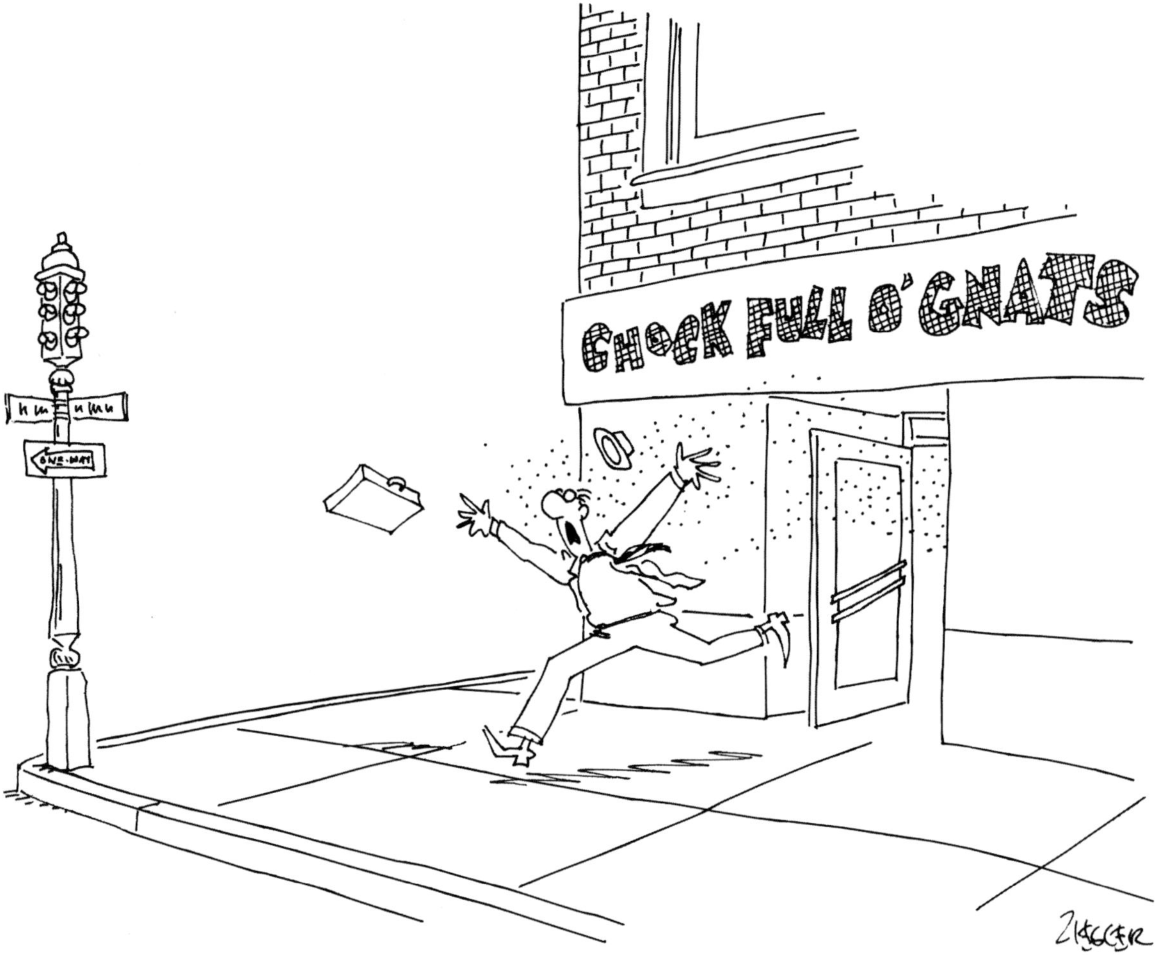
CHOCK FULL O' GNATS
ONE-WAY
ZIEGLER

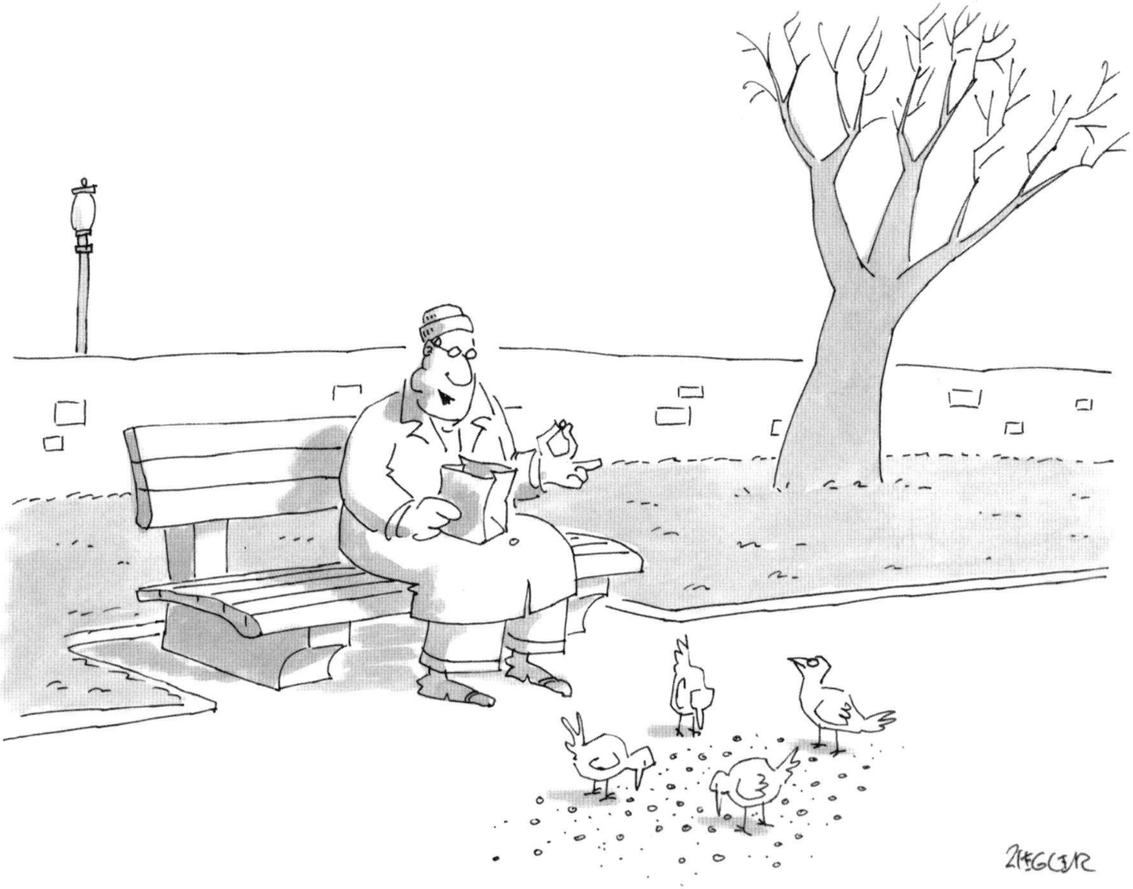
ZIEGLER

"You're right, these are good!"

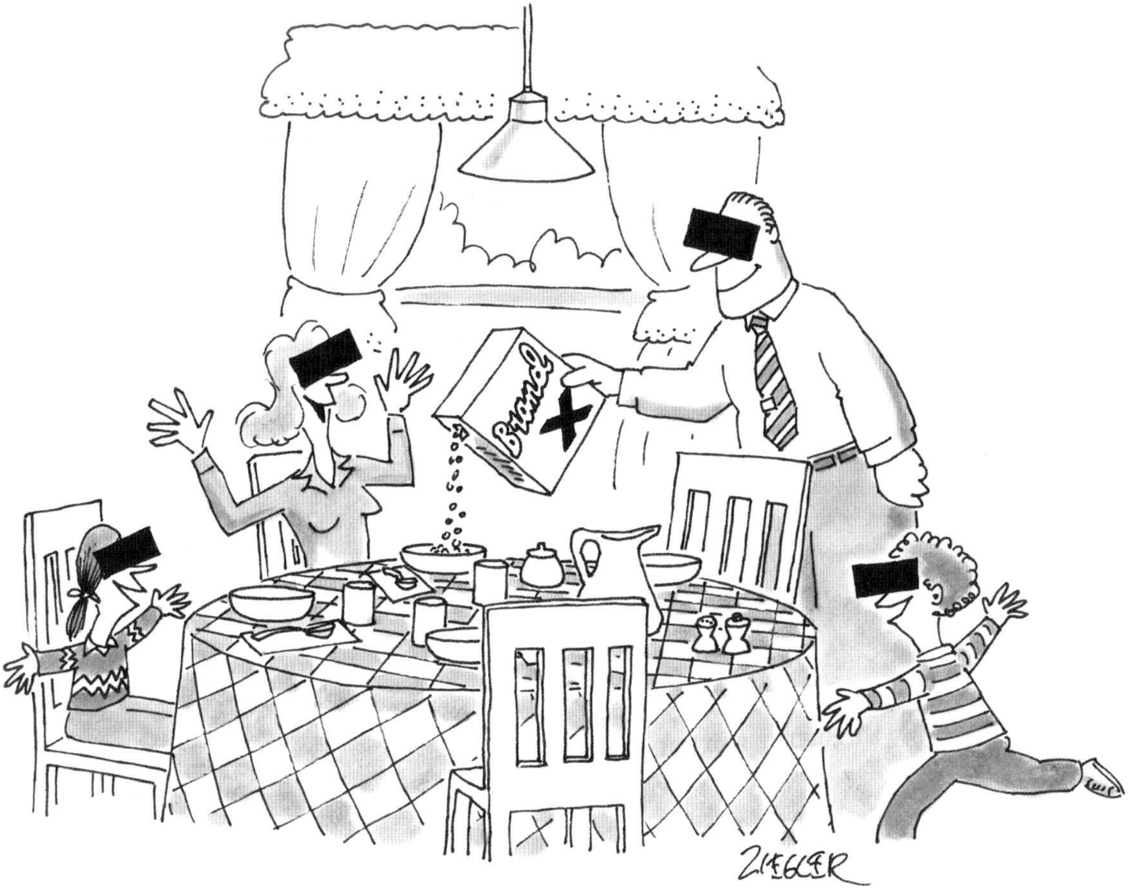
Brand X
ZIEGLER

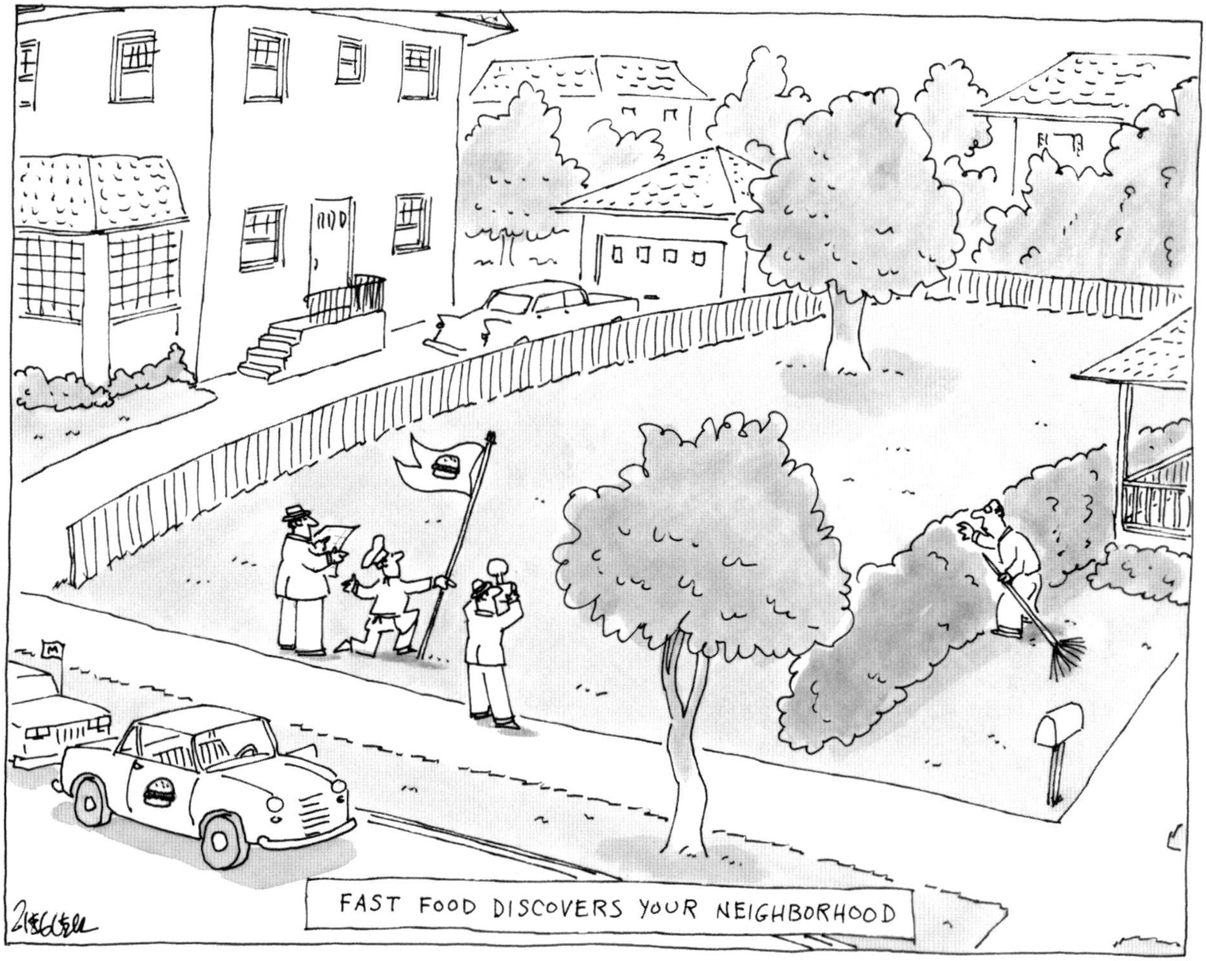
FAST FOOD DISCOVERS YOUR NEIGHBORHOOD

"To be perfectly honest, I've never ripped into anything that wasn't begging to be ripped into."

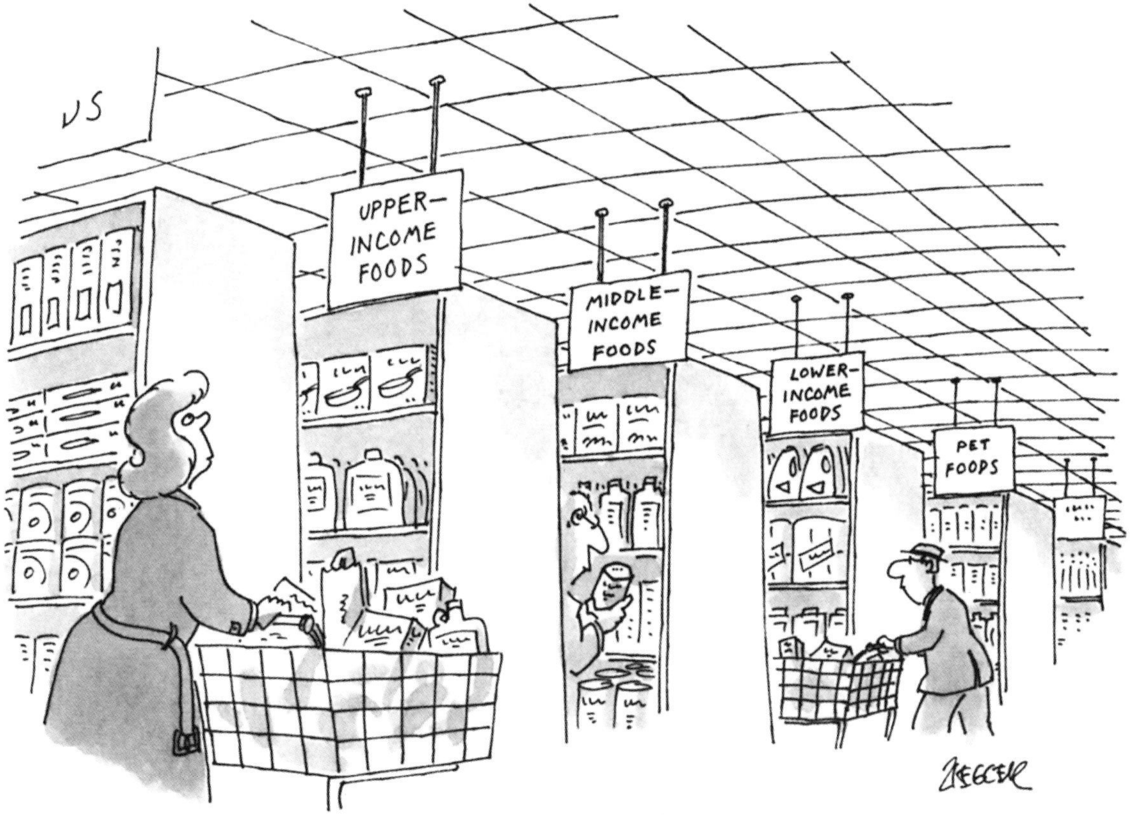
US
UPPER-
INCOME
FOODS
MIDDLE-
INCOME
FOODS
LOWER-
INCOME
FOODS
PET
FOODS
ZIEGLER

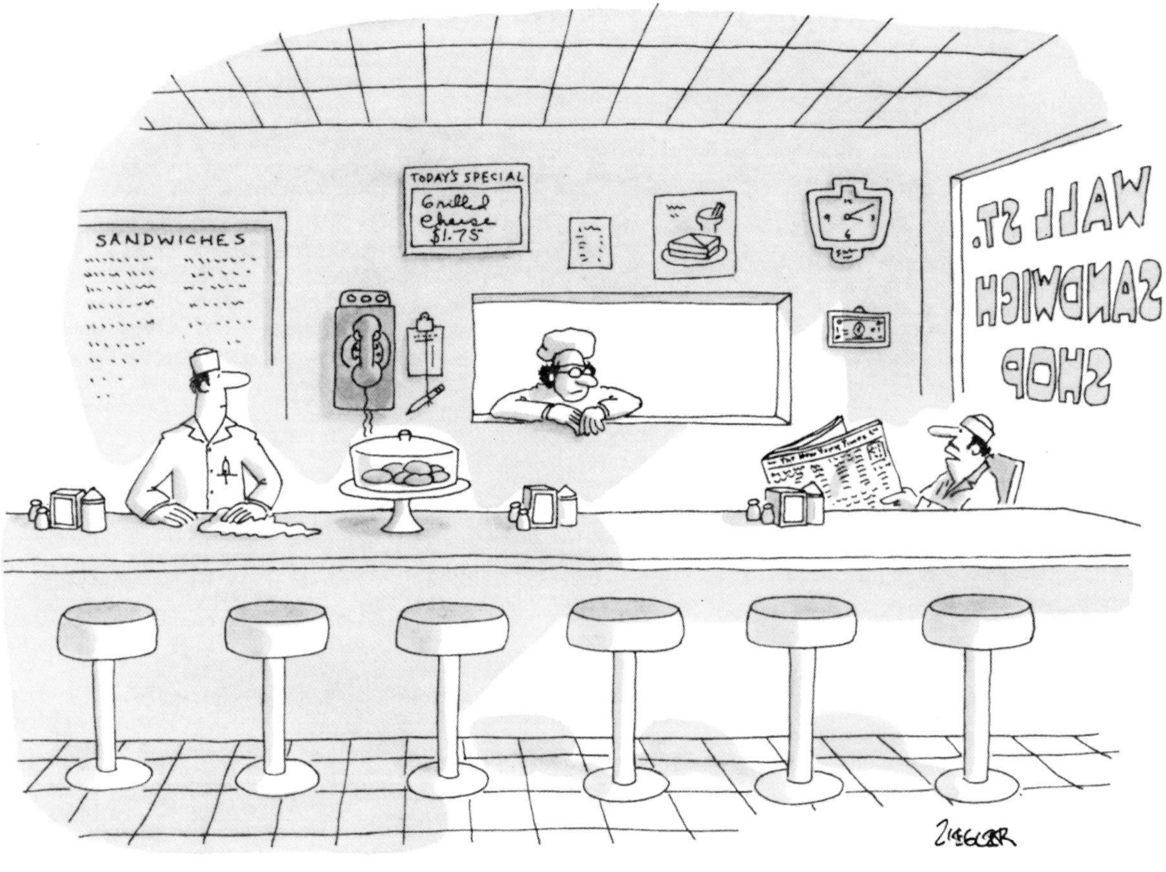
TODAY'S SPECIAL
Grilled Cheese $1.75
SANDWICHES
WALL ST. SANDWICH SHOP
ZIEGLER

"Liverwurst is down an eighth, egg-salad is up two and a half, and peanut-butter-and-jelly remains unchanged."

"*Virginia, please call The Pastry Shoppe and order me something evil.*"

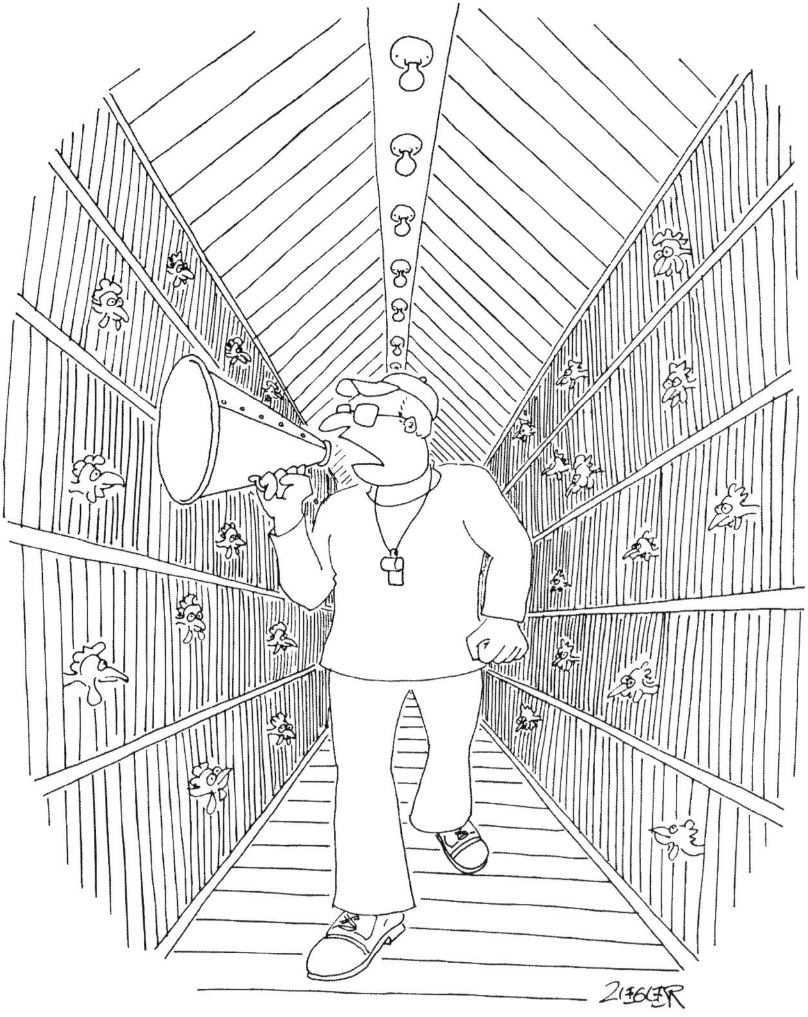
ZIEGLER

"I believe in eggs, and I think that you all believe in eggs, too!"

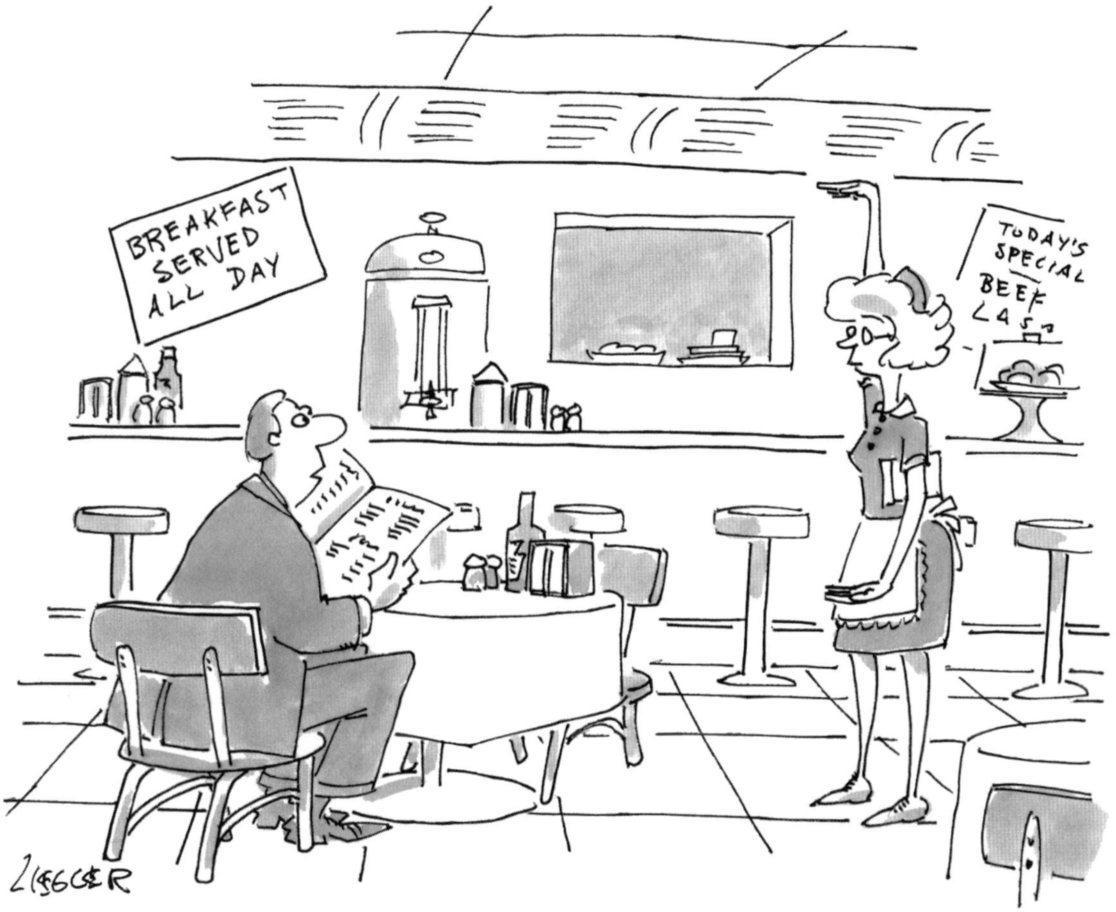
BREAKFAST SERVED ALL DAY
TODAY'S SPECIAL
BEEF
LAS

"In that case, I'll just have the short stack."

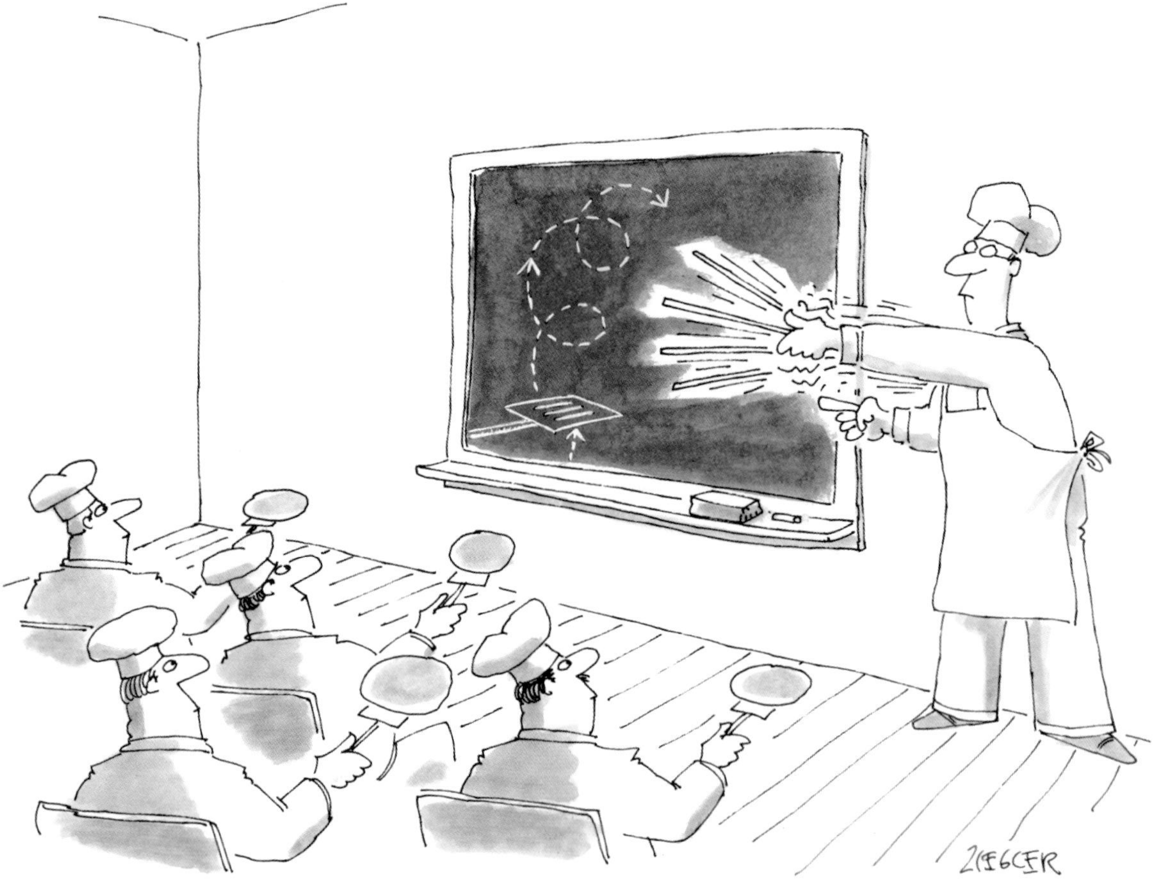
ZIEGLER

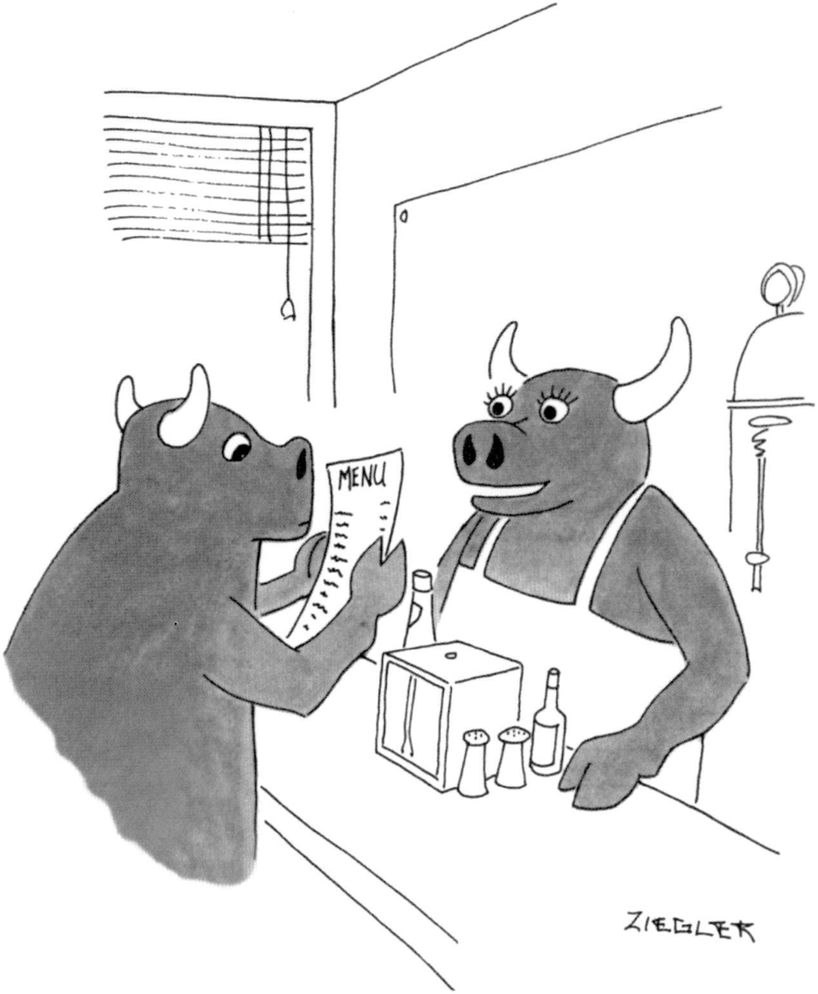
MENU
ZIEGLER

"Might I recommend the cud?"

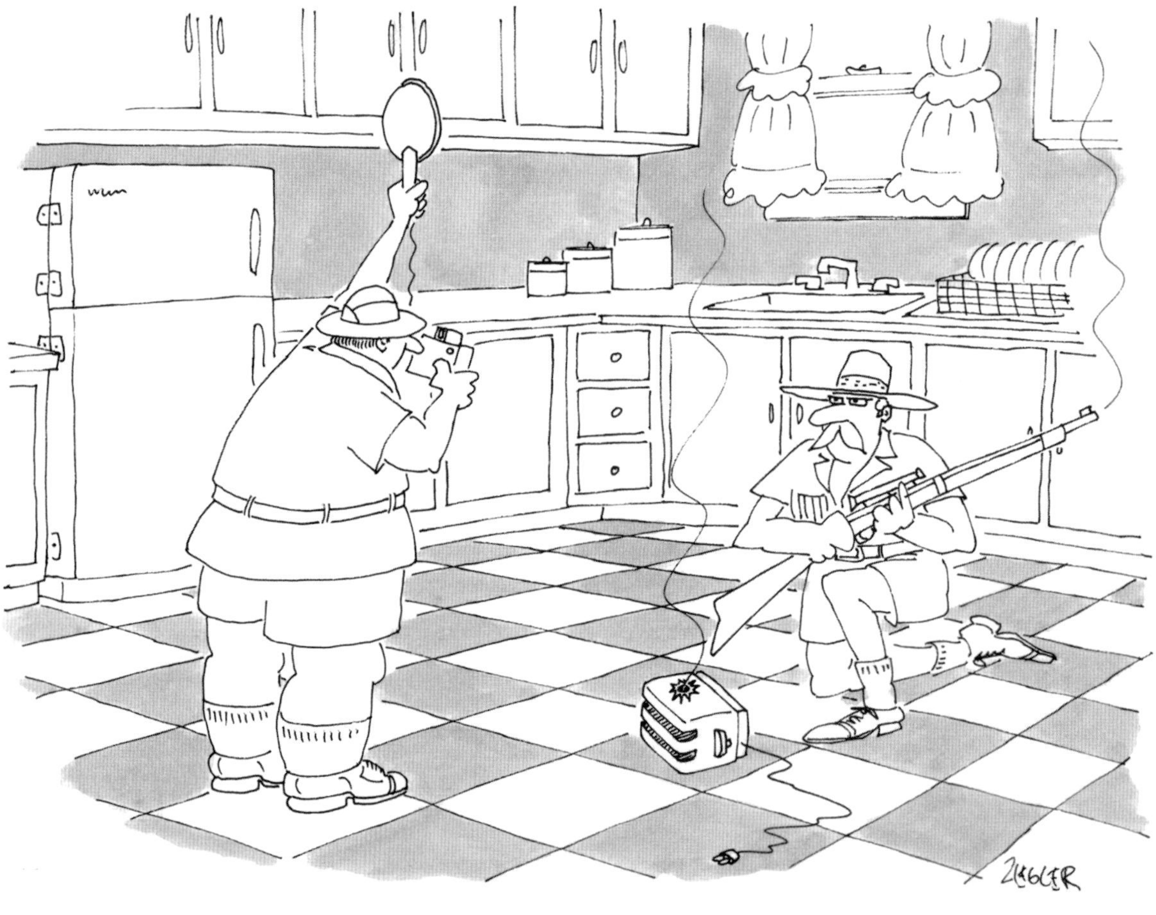
ZIEGLER

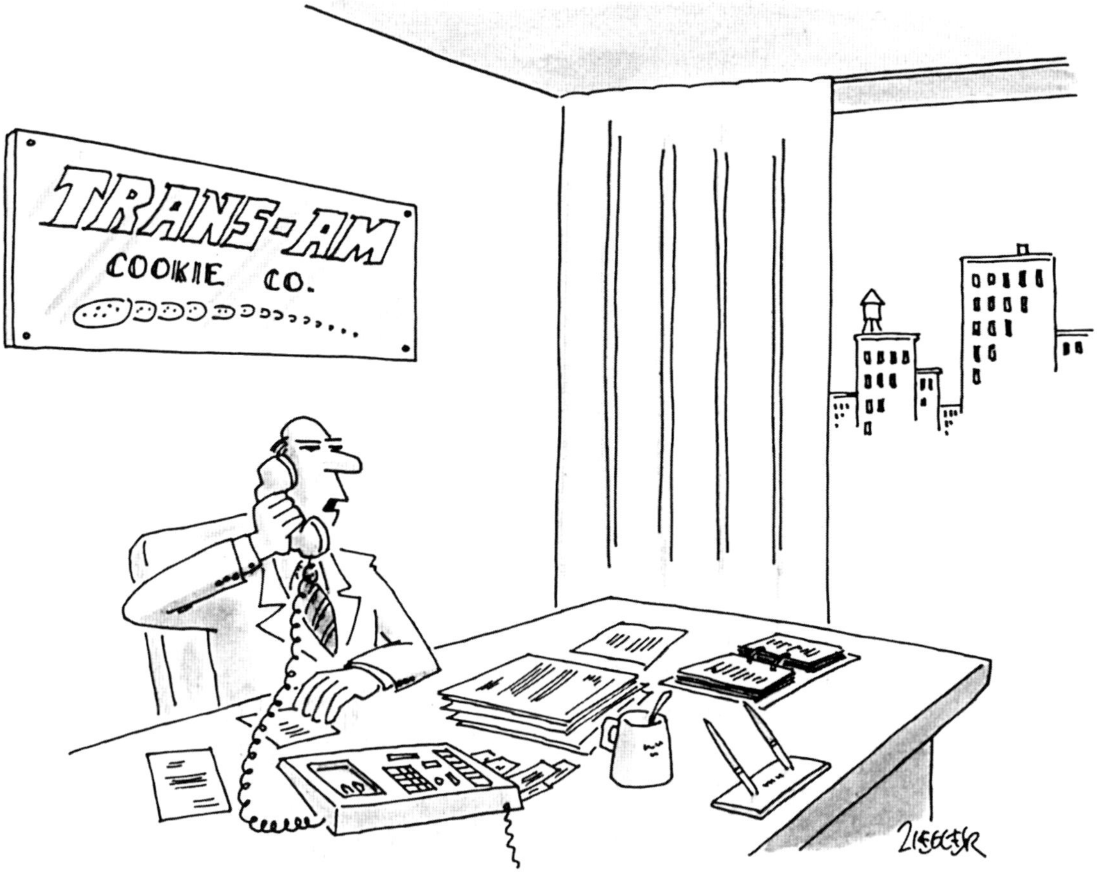
TRANS-AM
COOKIE CO.
ZIEGLER

"Sorry, Bob, but we'll have to cancel tomorrow's lunch.
I'm summiting all week with the boys from Amalgamated Chocolate Chip."

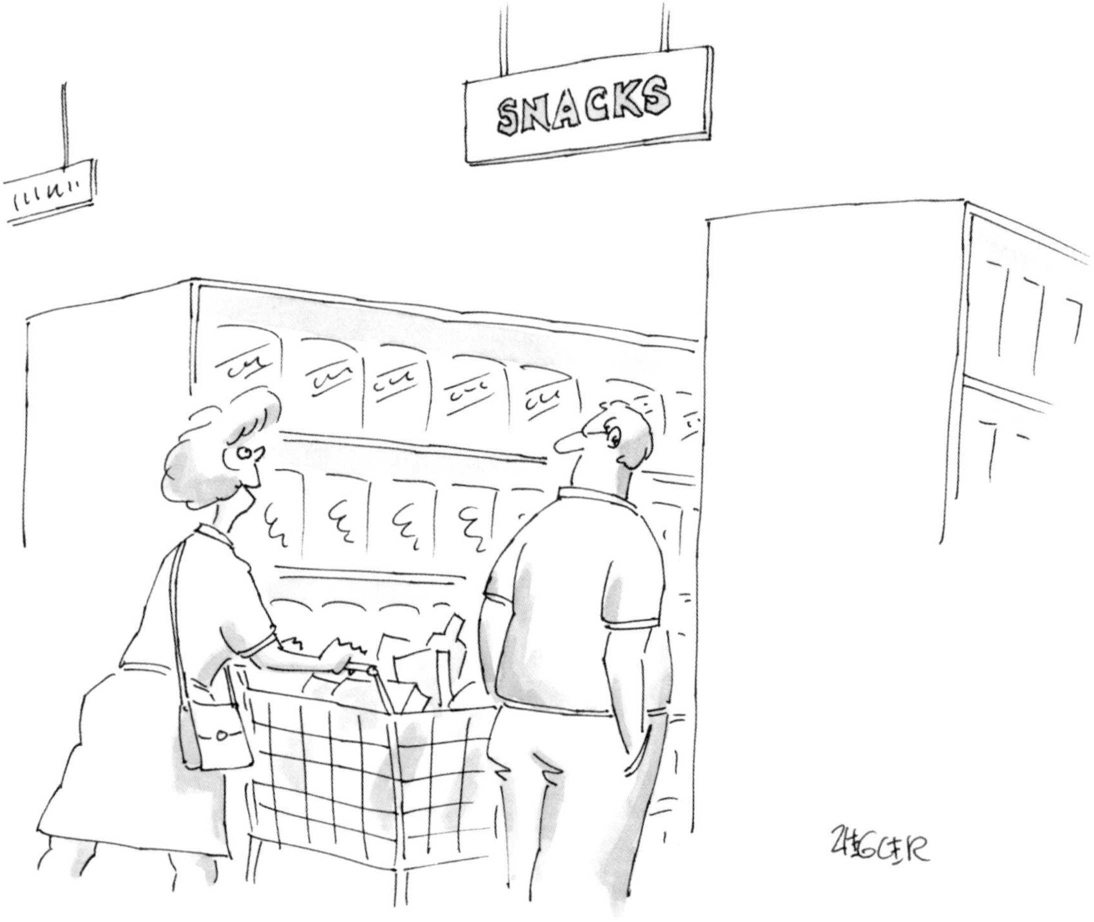
SNACKS
ZIEGLER

"I love this aisle with its bright and welcoming packages half-filled with air. Snacks! It even sounds dietary."

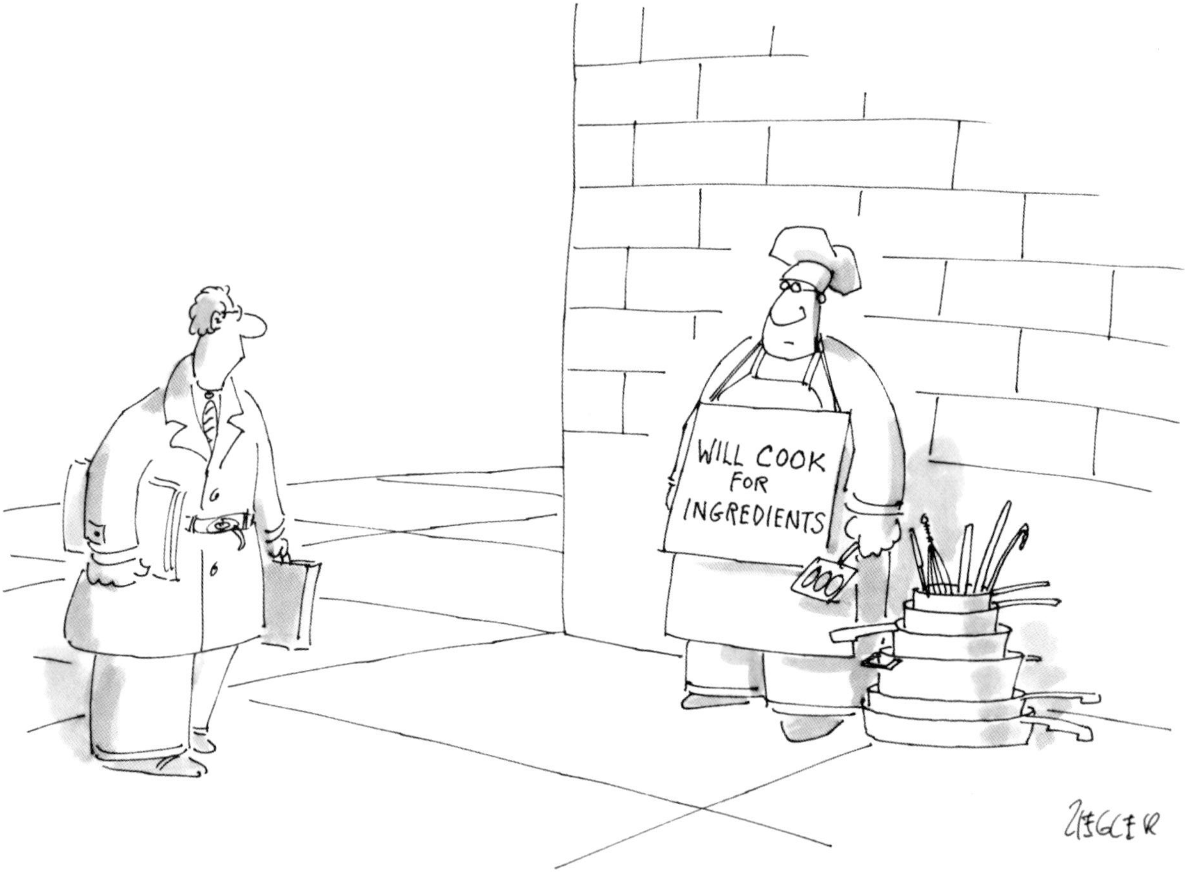
WILL COOK
FOR
INGREDIENTS
ZIEGLER

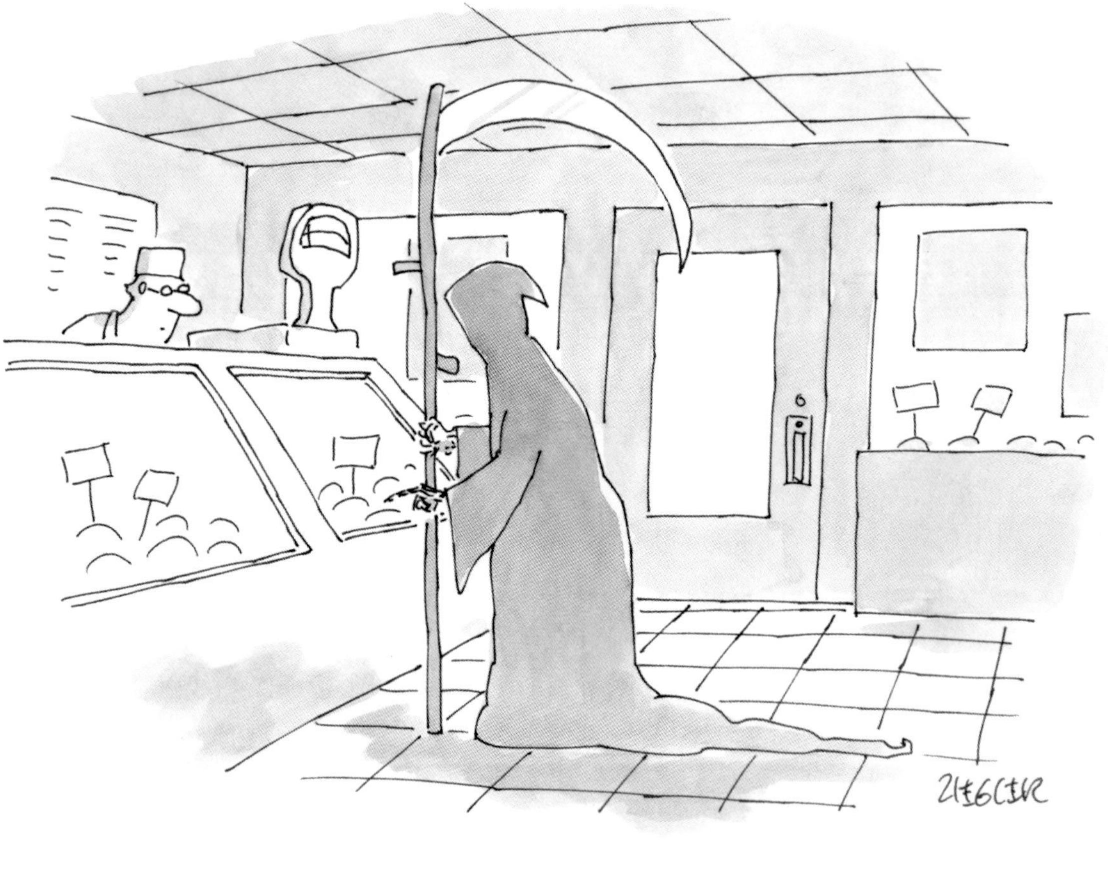
ZIEGLER

"That dead thing in the corner looks good."

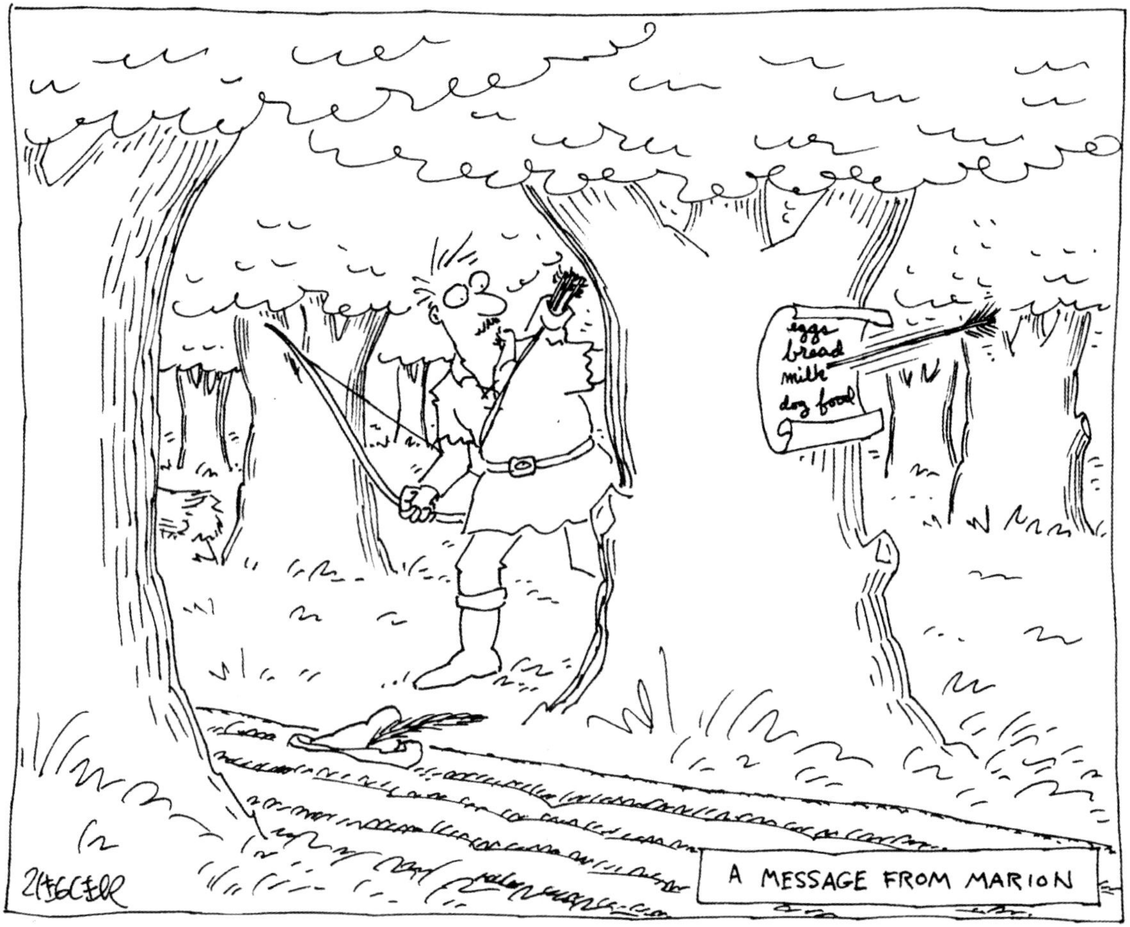
eggs
bread
milk
dog food
ZIEGLER
A MESSAGE FROM MARION

"*Your constant cries to cut the pork sadden me, Senator.*"

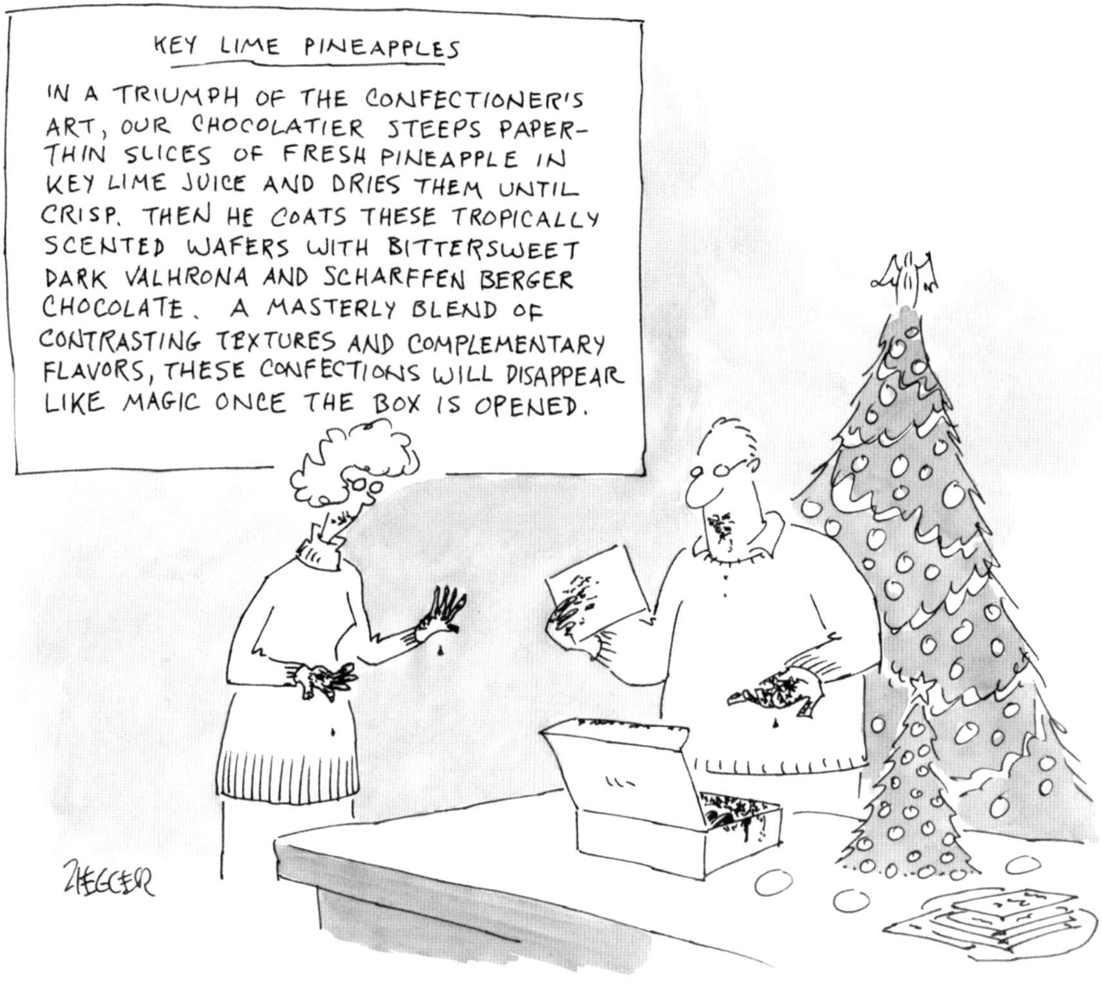
KEY LIME PINEAPPLES
IN A TRIUMPH OF THE CONFECTIONER'S ART, OUR CHOCOLATIER STEEPS PAPER-THIN SLICES OF FRESH PINEAPPLE IN KEY LIME JUICE AND DRIES THEM UNTIL CRISP. THEN HE COATS THESE TROPICALLY SCENTED WAFERS WITH BITTERSWEET DARK VALHRONA AND SCHARFFEN BERGER CHOCOLATE. A MASTERLY BLEND OF CONTRASTING TEXTURES AND COMPLEMENTARY FLAVORS, THESE CONFECTIONS WILL DISAPPEAR LIKE MAGIC ONCE THE BOX IS OPENED.
ZIEGLER

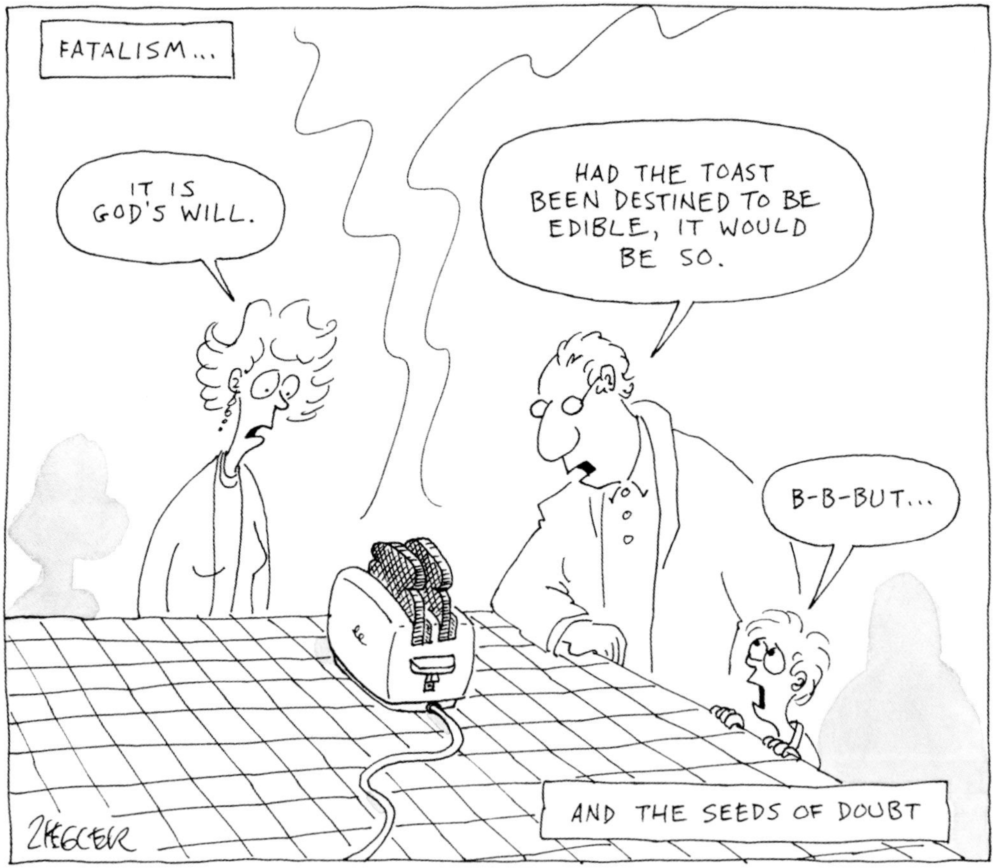
FATALISM...
IT IS GOD'S WILL.
HAD THE TOAST BEEN DESTINED TO BE EDIBLE, IT WOULD BE SO.
B-B-BUT...
AND THE SEEDS OF DOUBT
ZIEGLER

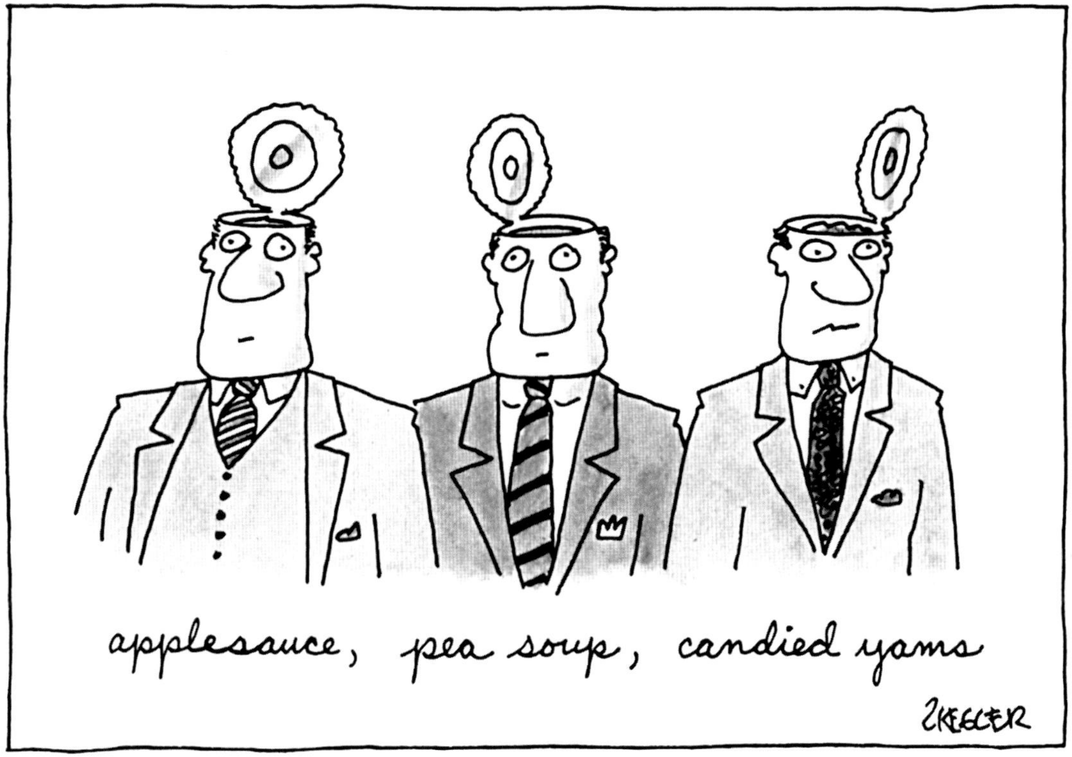
applesauce, pea soup, candied yams
ZIEGLER

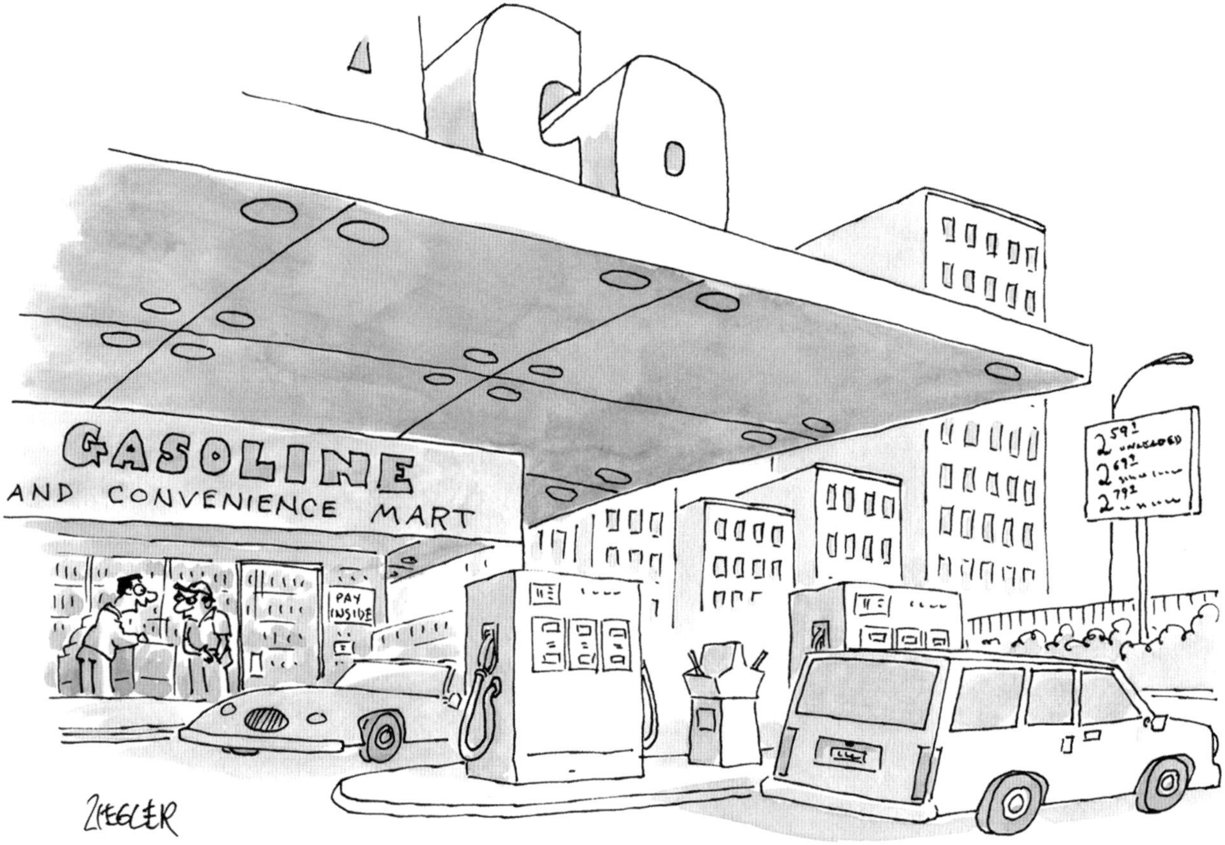
GASOLINE
AND CONVENIENCE MART
PAY INSIDE
ZIEGLER

"The good news is that a delicious stick of jerky is still a very affordable seventy-five cents."

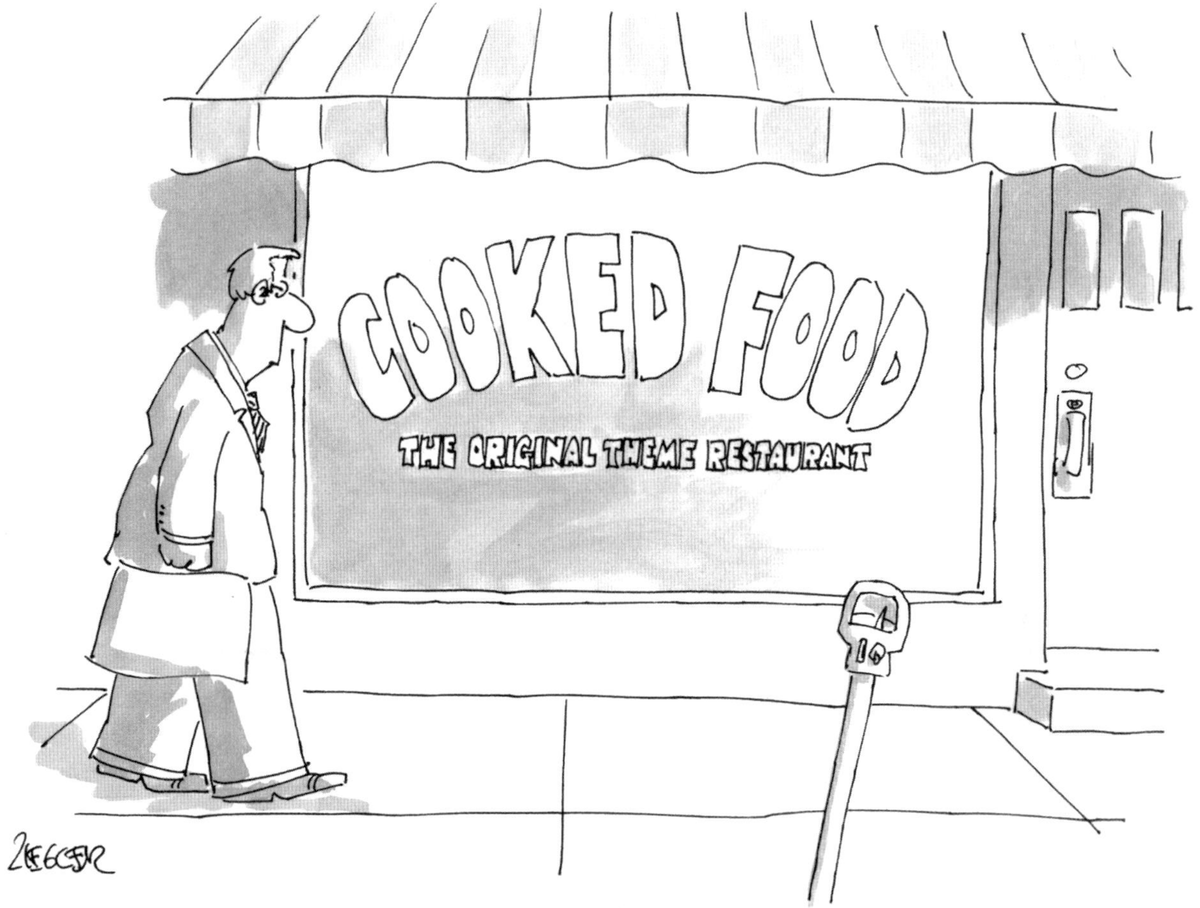
COOKED FOOD
THE ORIGINAL THEME RESTAURANT
ZIEGLER

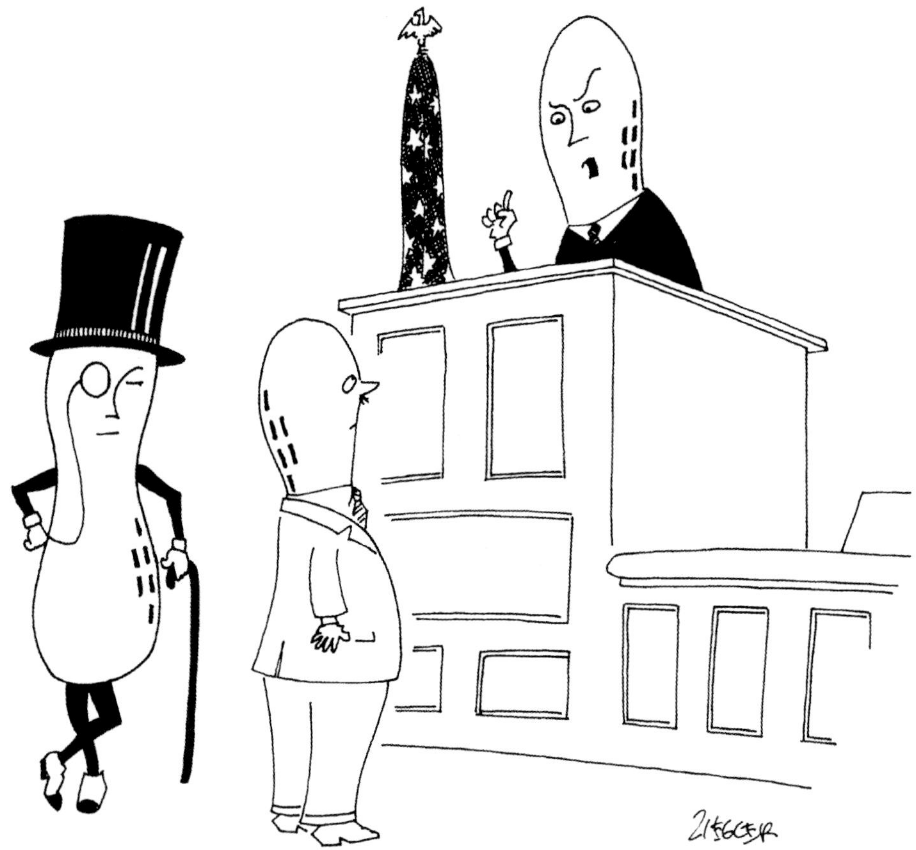
ZIEGLER

"Counselor will instruct his client to remove his hat and put on some pants before sentencing."

"Yes, but take away the rodent droppings and the occasional shard of glass, and you've still got a damn fine product."

"Has it ever occurred to you just to say,
'Hey, I quit. I don't want to be a part of the food chain anymore'?"

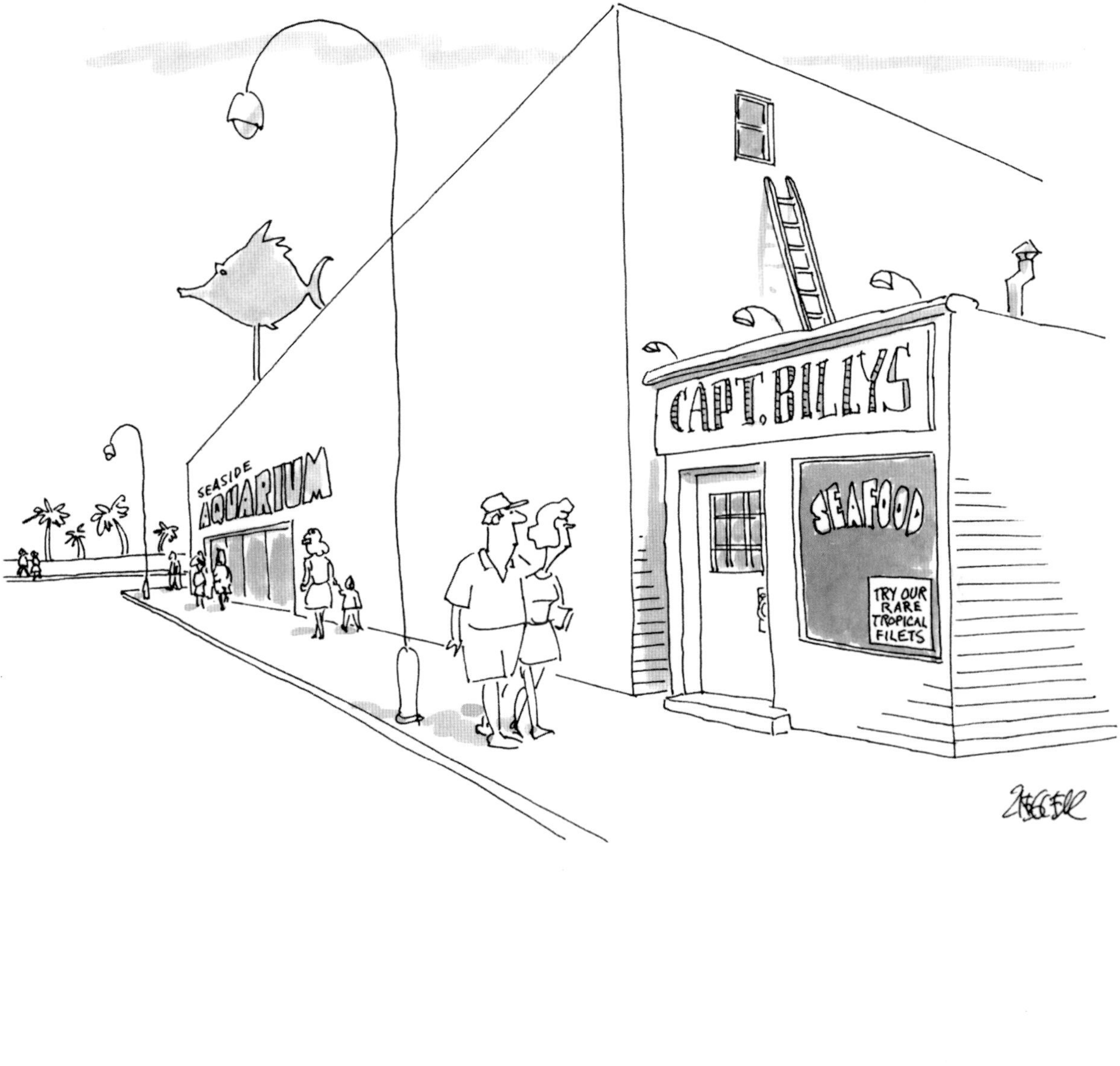
CAPT. BILLYS
SEAFOOD
TRY OUR RARE TROPICAL FILETS
SEASIDE AQUARIUM

"You'd be a mad cow, too, if you just found out that McDonald's has sold over seventeen zillion hamburgers."

"Lunchward ho!"

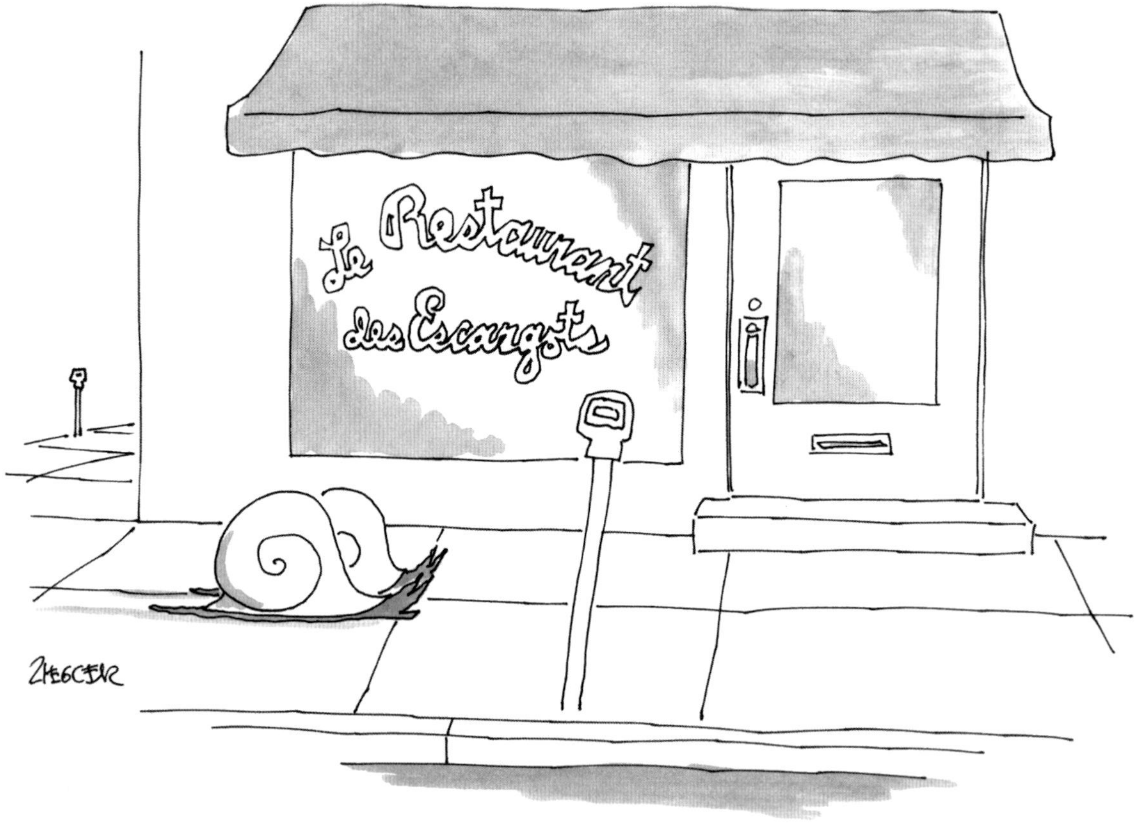
Le Restaurant
des Escargots
ZIEGLER

"Ooh, look—French! Let's try it!"

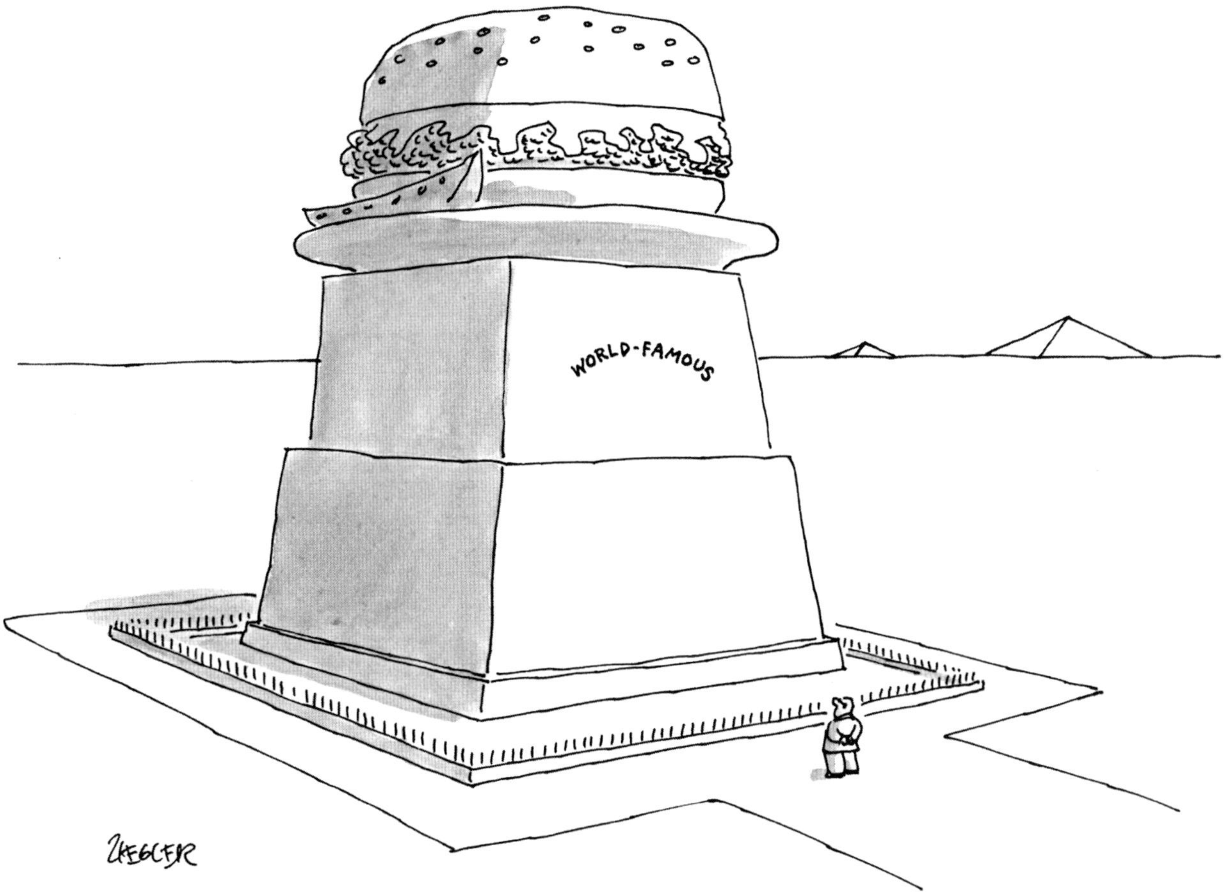
WORLD-FAMOUS
ZIEGLER

PEANUT BUTTER...

AND JELLY...

SANDWICH!

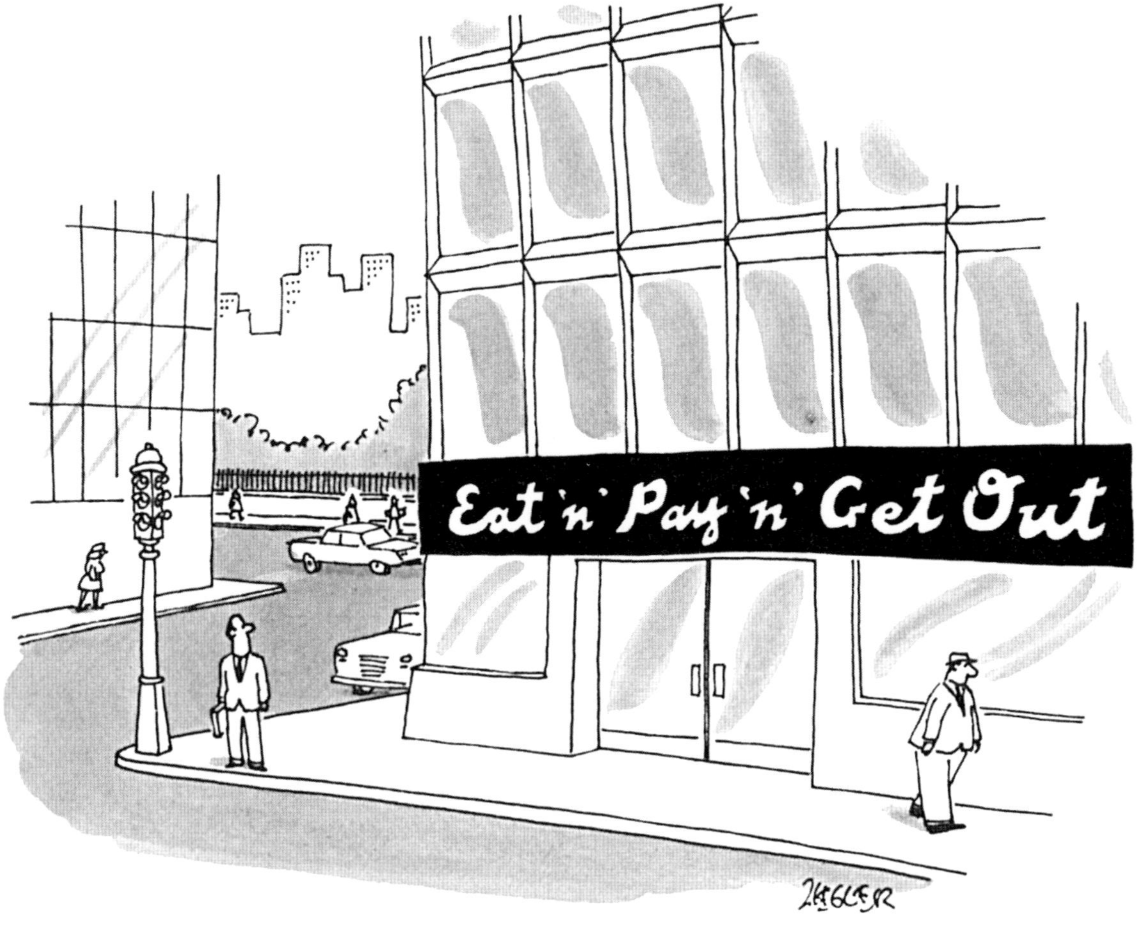
Eat 'n' Pay 'n' Get Out

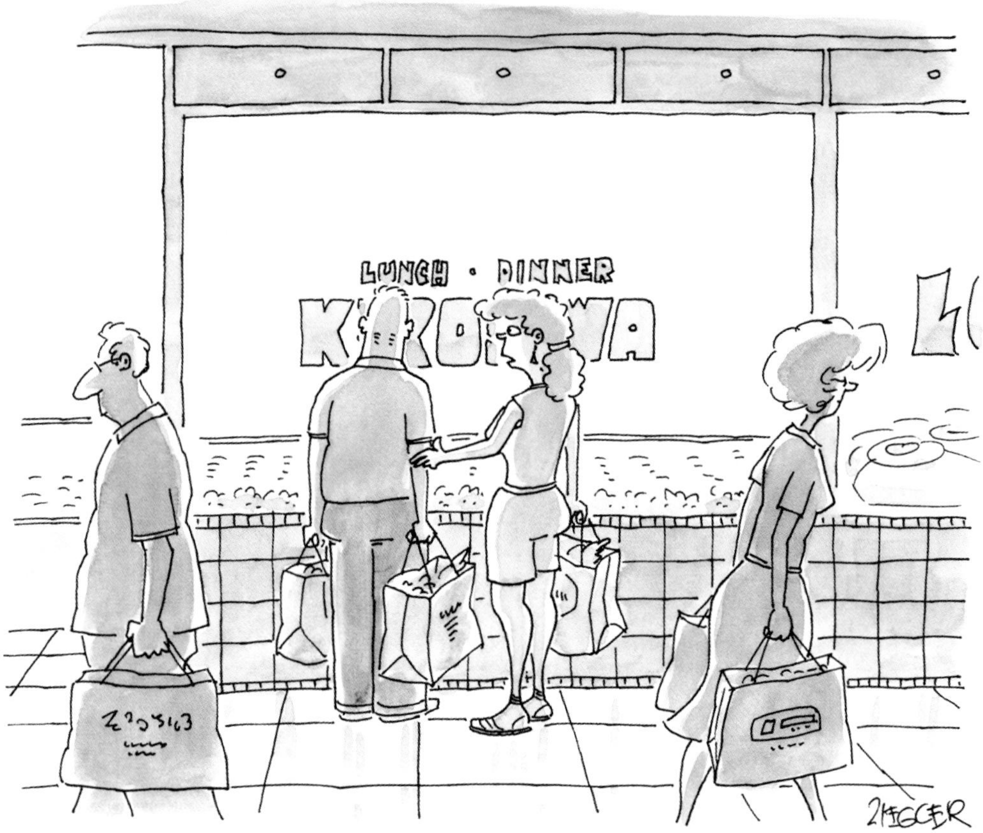
LUNCH · DINNER
ZIEGLER

"One of us has to draw the line somewhere, and I draw the line at mall sushi."

"*The booths are for parties of four or more.*"

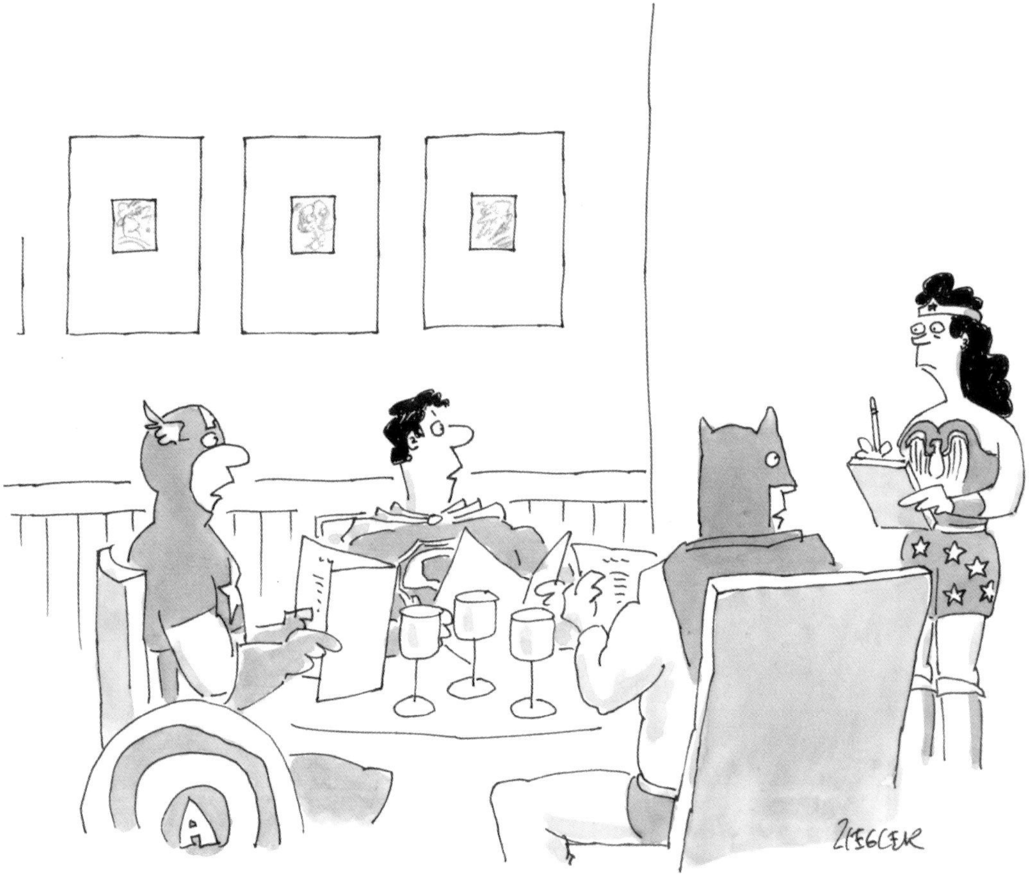
ZIEGLER

"What th—???"

"Two burgers, two fries, two martinis—and we'll have those to go."

"I can offer you a donut or something cold
while the cook is completing his controlled burn."

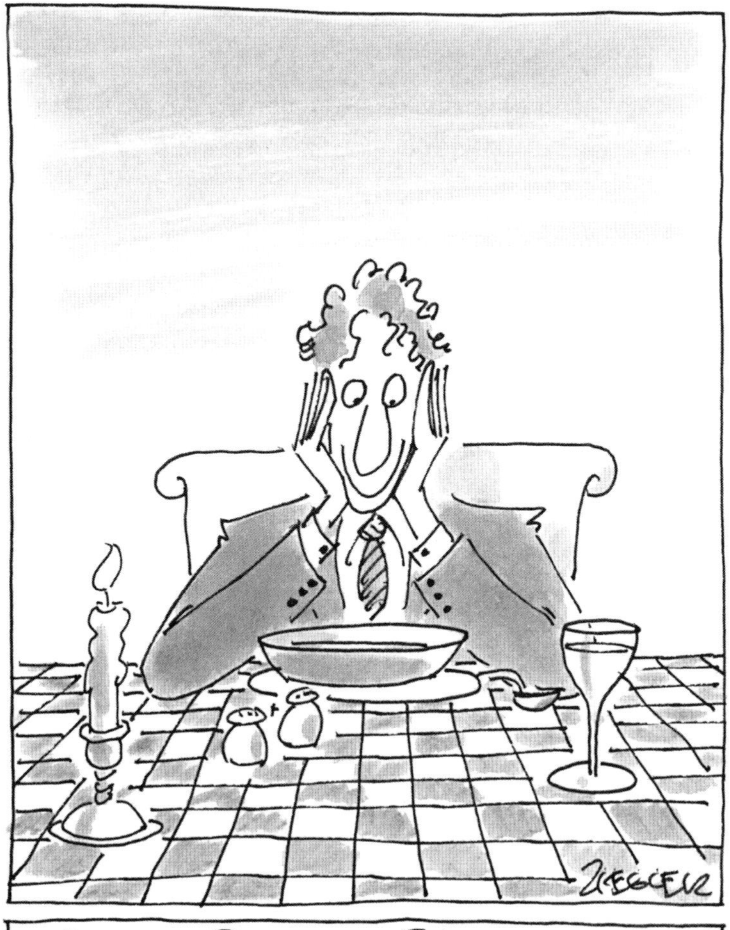
ZIEGLER

The Bisque Narcissus

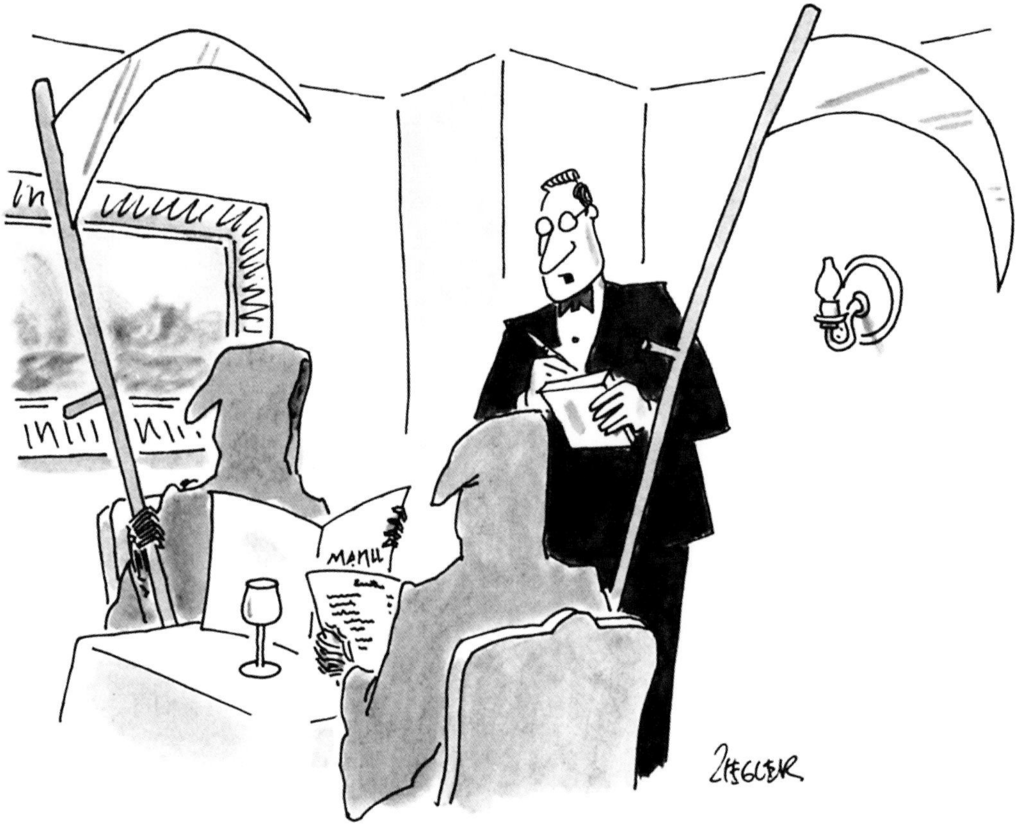
MENU
ZIEGLER

"The Pasta Muerta is very good today."

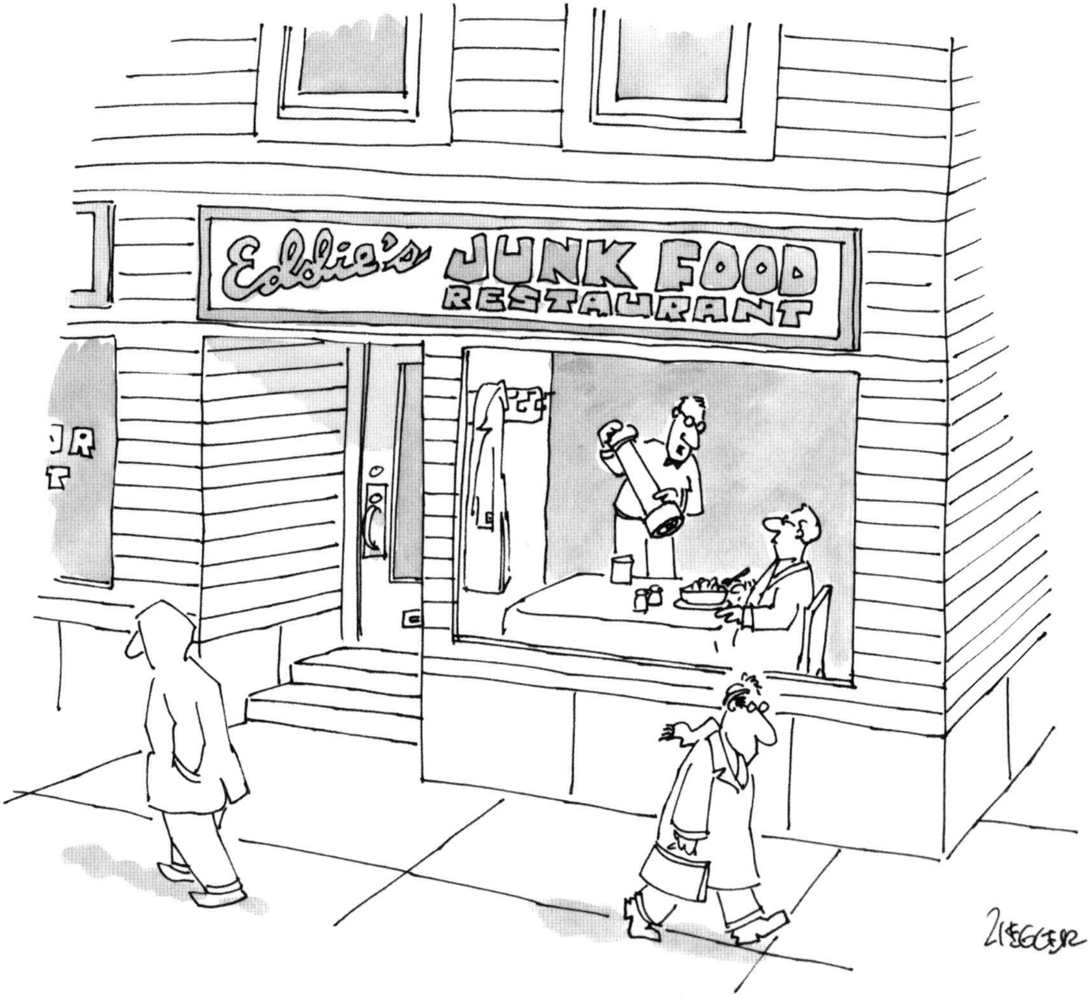
Eddie's JUNK FOOD RESTAURANT
ZIEGLER

"Fresh-ground Cheez-Its on those Mallomars, sir?"

"*From right to left, you have your tekkamaki, your futomaki, and then your yamaimo roll. The little pile of pink stuff is ginger, the green one's wasabi. And, of course, you already recognize your vodka Martini.*"

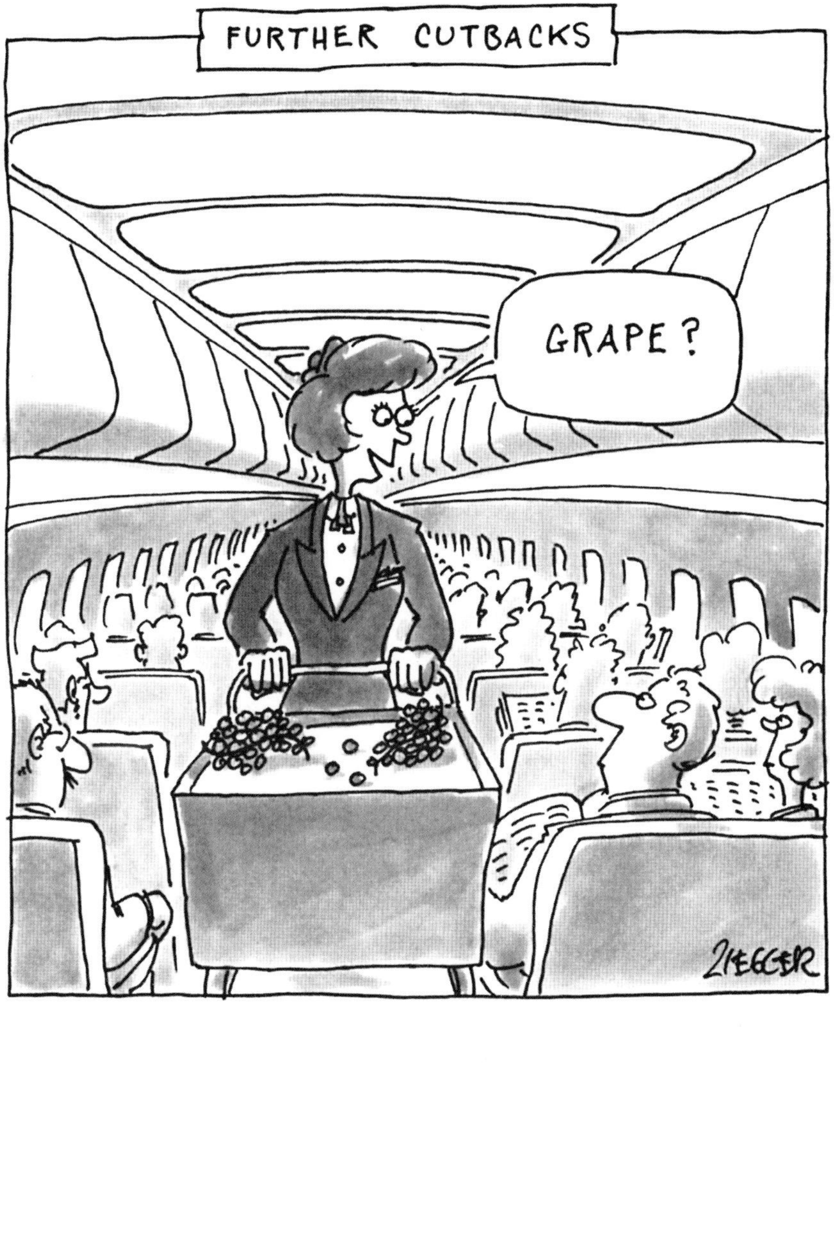
FURTHER CUTBACKS
GRAPE?
ZIEGLER

"I'll have what everyone else is having."

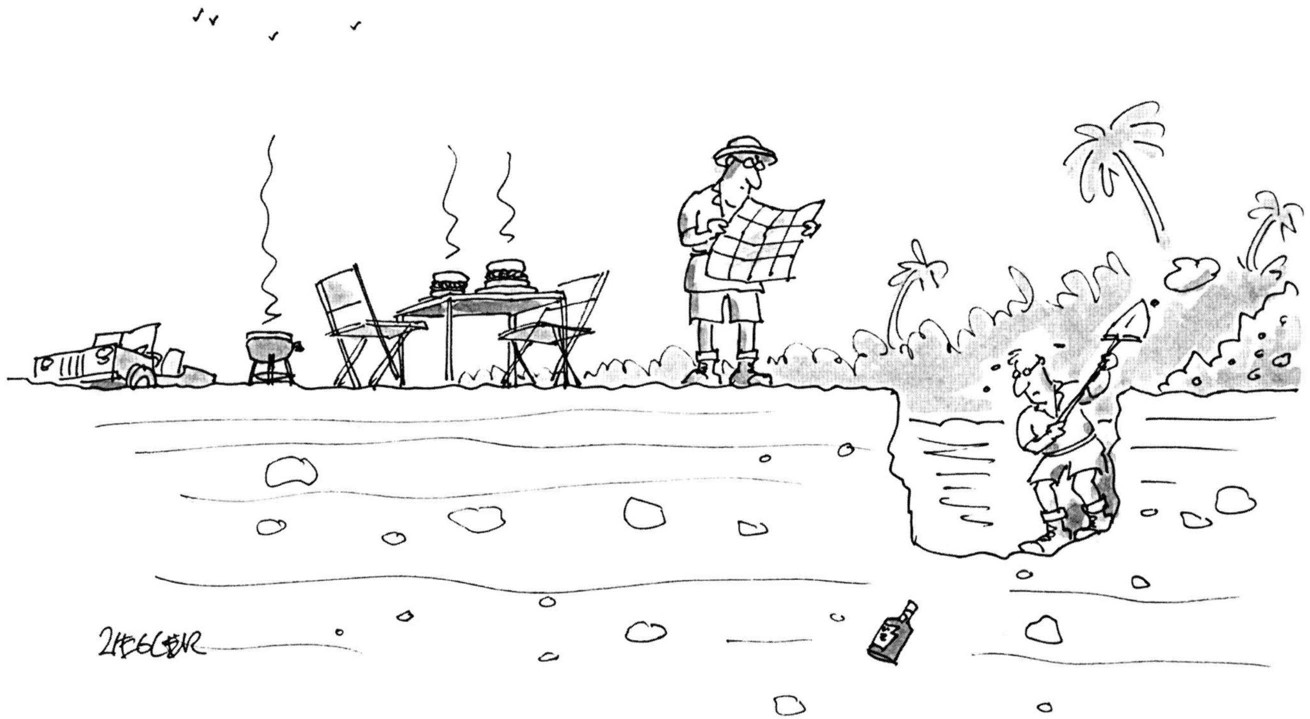
ZIEGLER

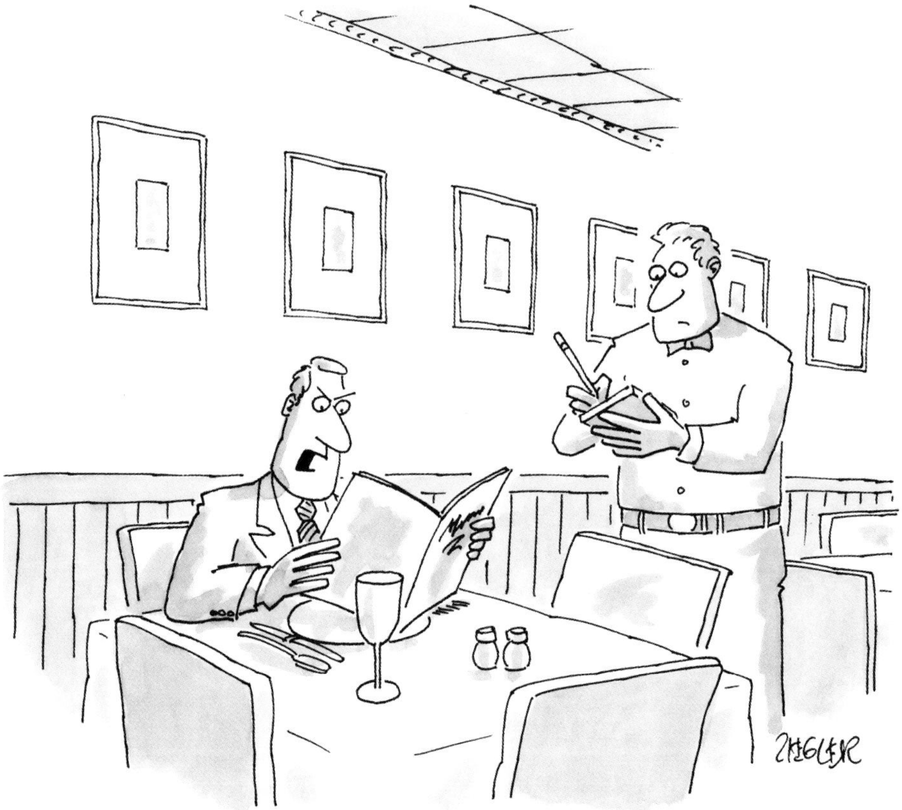
ZIEGLER

"I'll have the misspelled 'Ceasar' salad and the improperly hyphenated veal osso-buco."

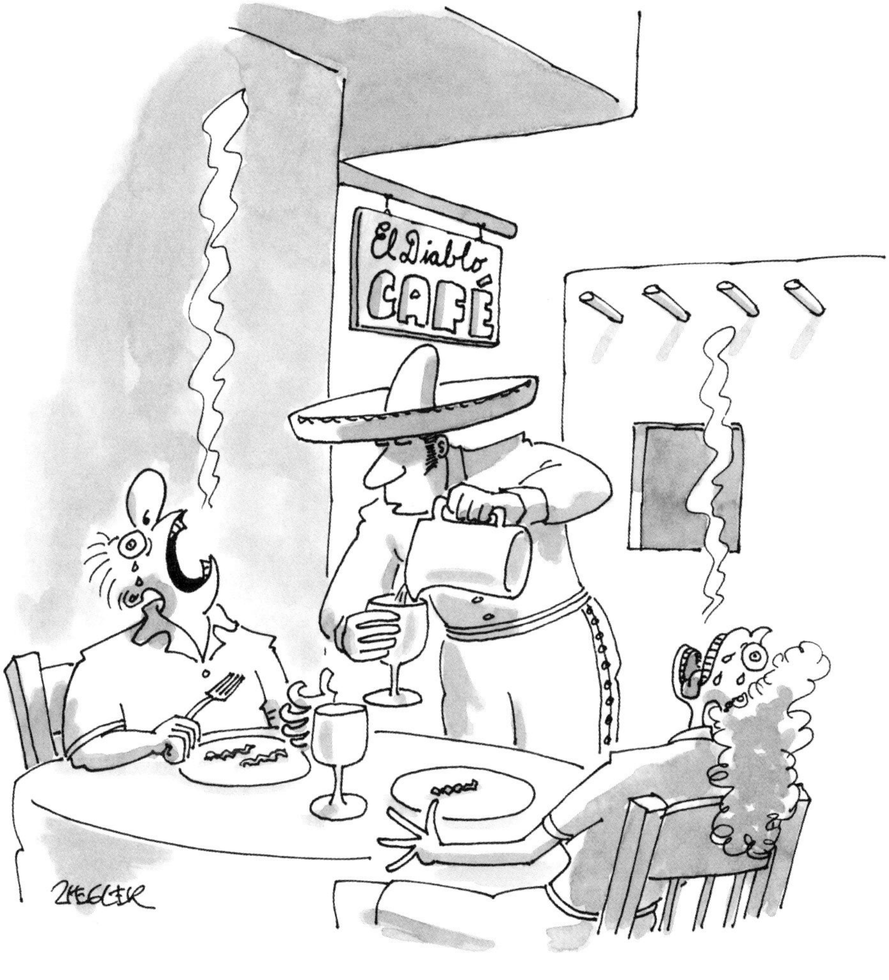
El Diablo
CAFÉ

"Más agua for the gringos?"

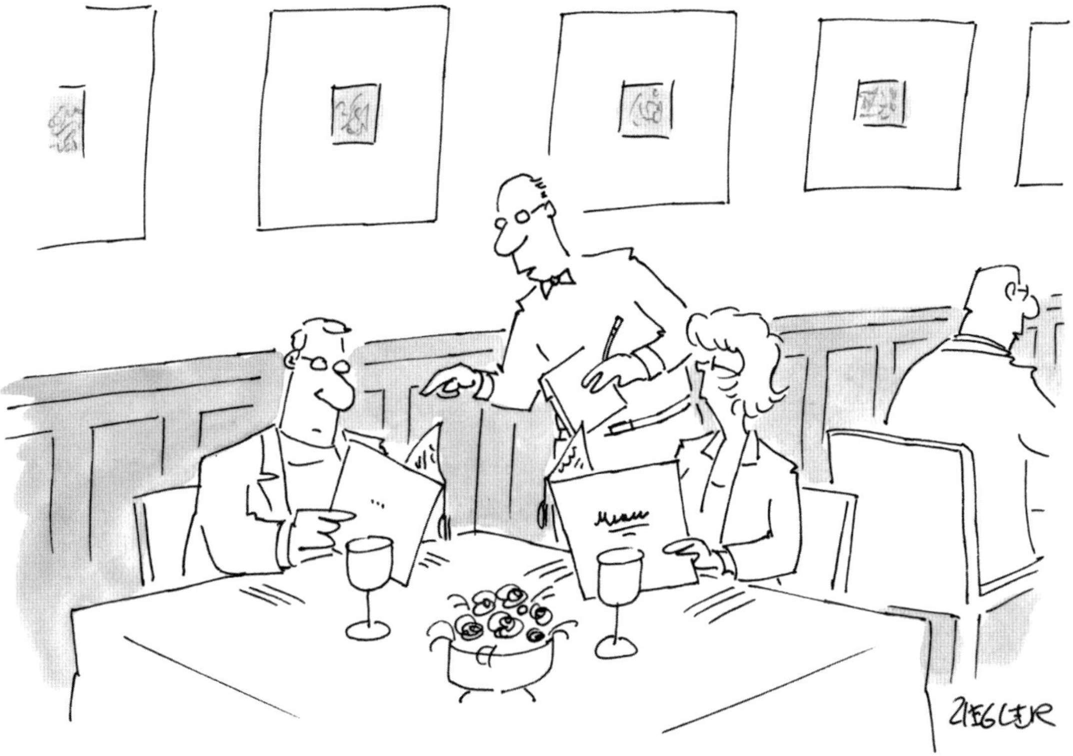
Menu
ZIEGLER

"I wonder if you folks are aware that black cod is this year's Chilean sea bass."

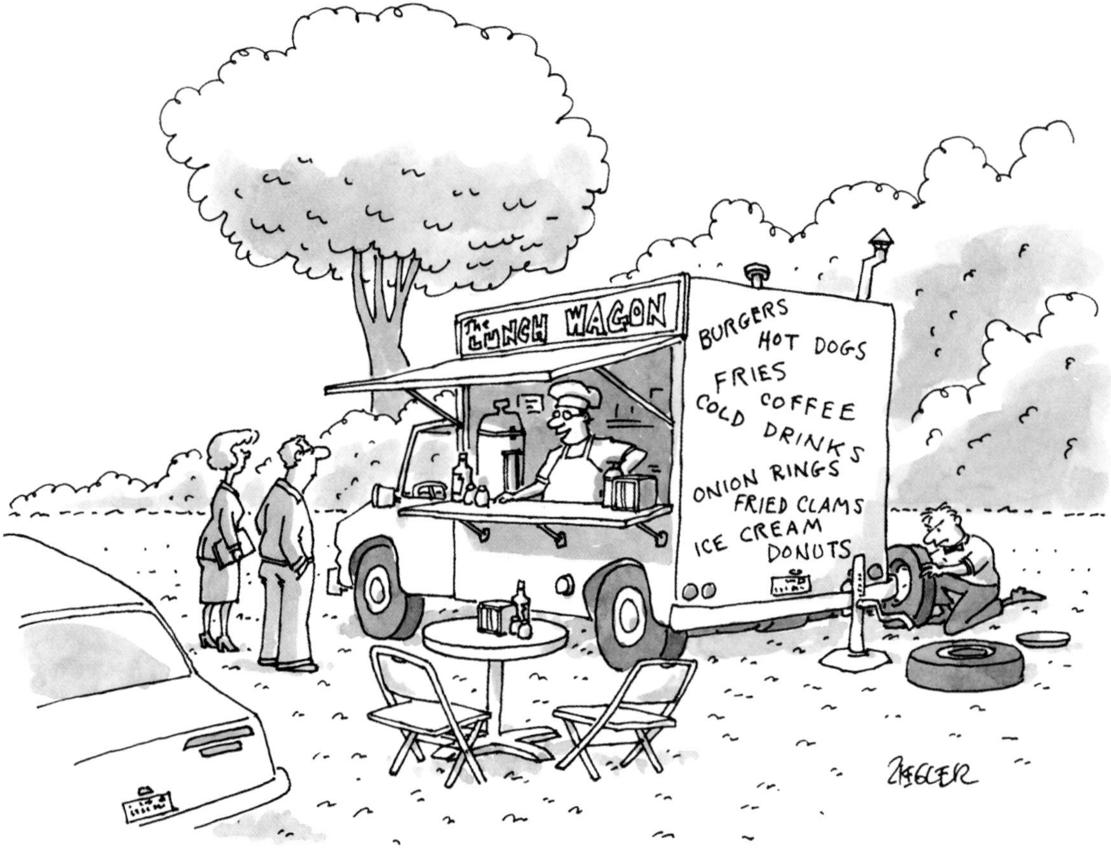
The LUNCH WAGON
BURGERS
HOT DOGS
FRIES
COFFEE
COLD DRINKS
ONION RINGS
FRIED CLAMS
ICE CREAM
DONUTS
ZIEGLER

"If you would care to take a seat, our waiter, Paul, will be with you momentarily."

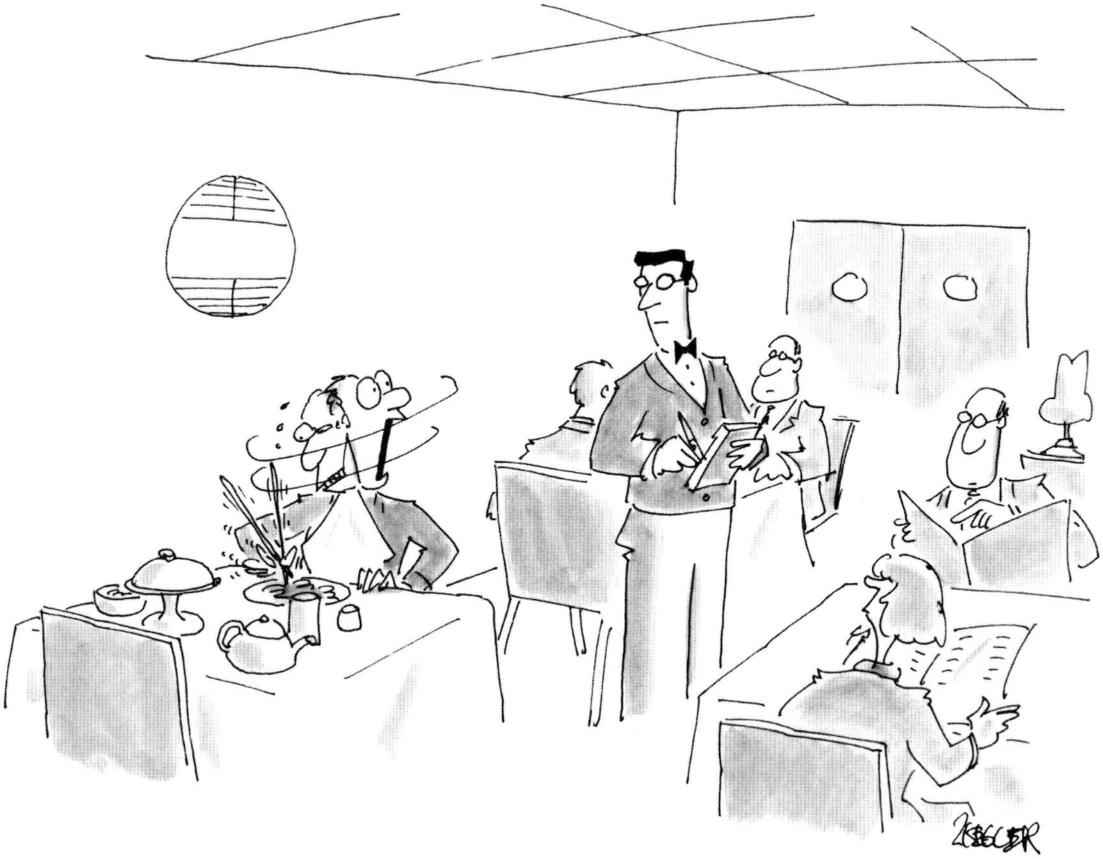
KOREN

"They won't work!!!"

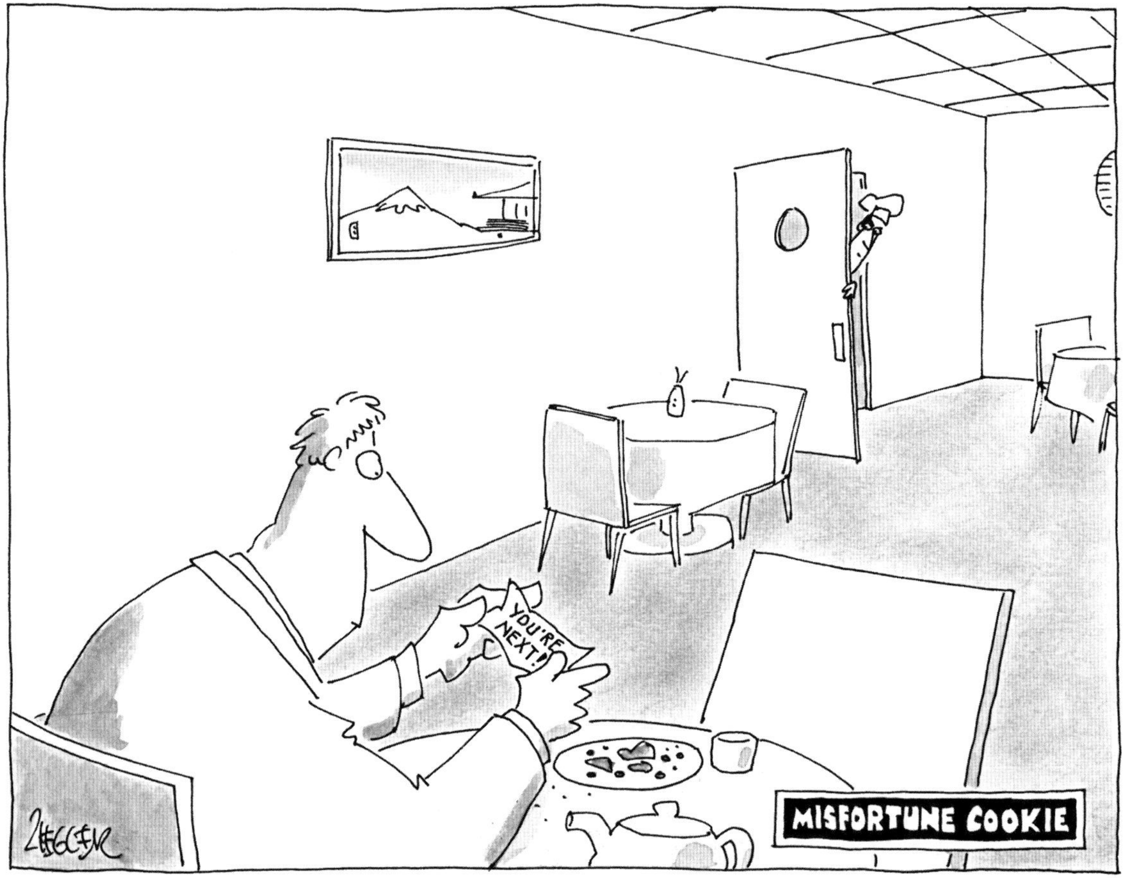
YOU'RE NEXT!
MISFORTUNE COOKIE

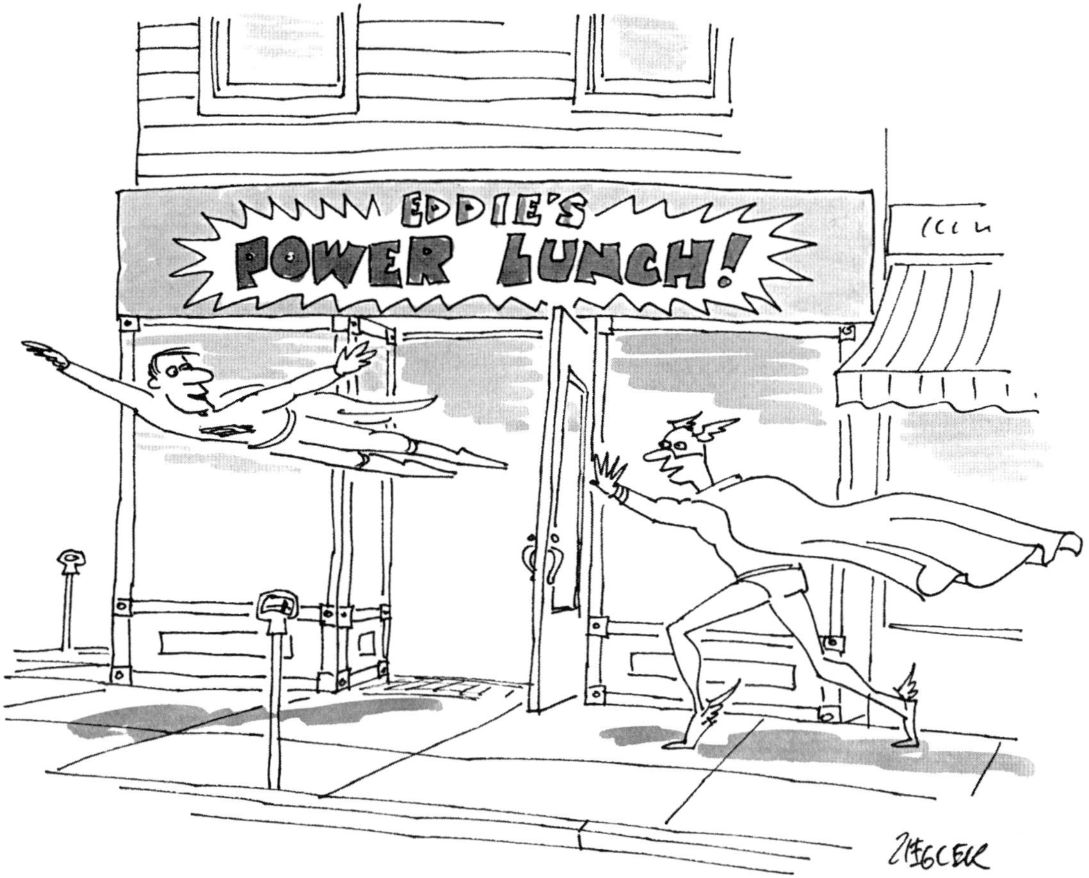
EDDIE'S
POWER LUNCH!
ZIEGLER

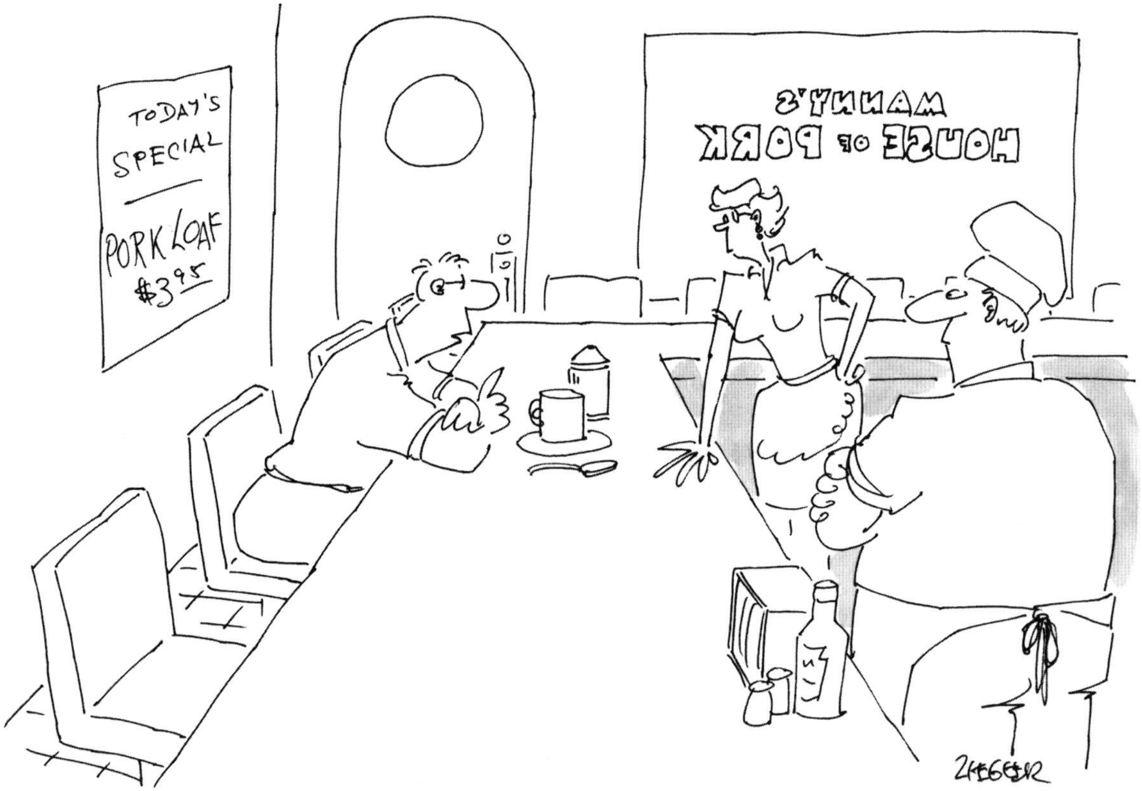
TODAY'S SPECIAL
PORK LOAF $3.95
MANNY'S HOUSE OF PORK
ZIEGLER

"Let's face it. All the adventure is gone since they went and bred all the trichinosis out of it."

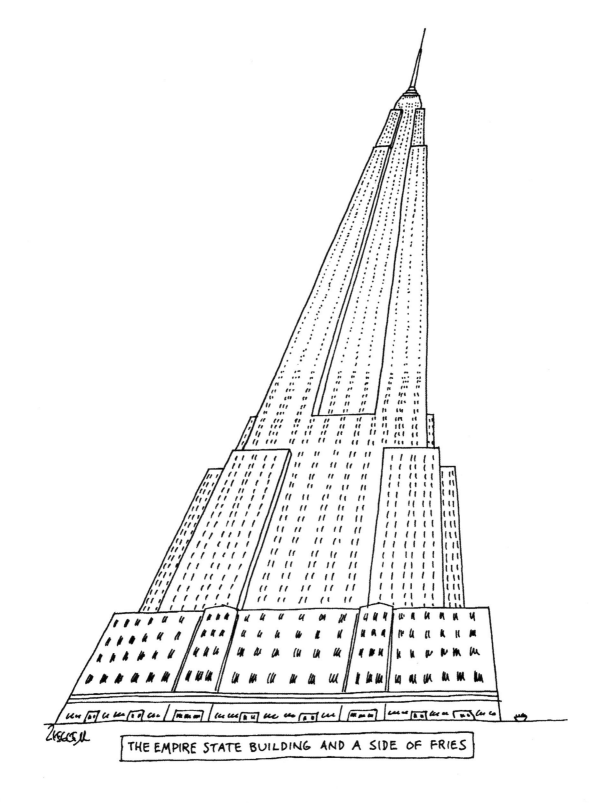

THE EMPIRE STATE BUILDING AND A SIDE OF FRIES

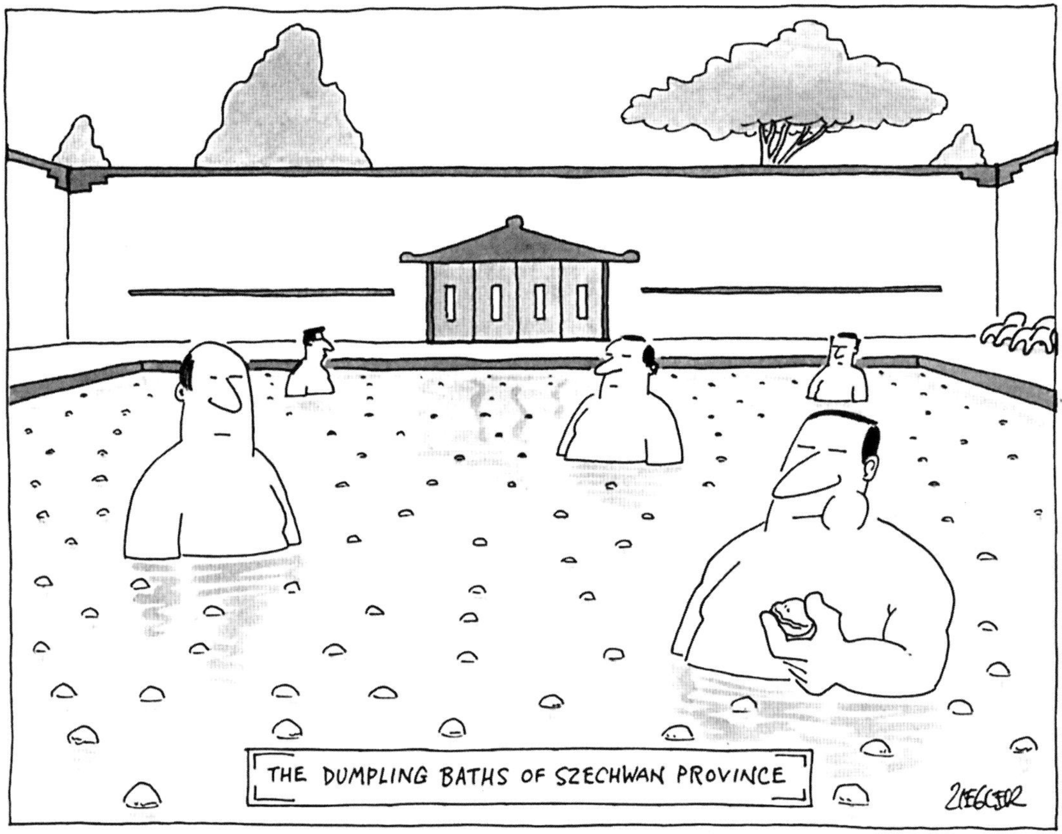
THE DUMPLING BATHS OF SZECHWAN PROVINCE
ZIEGLER

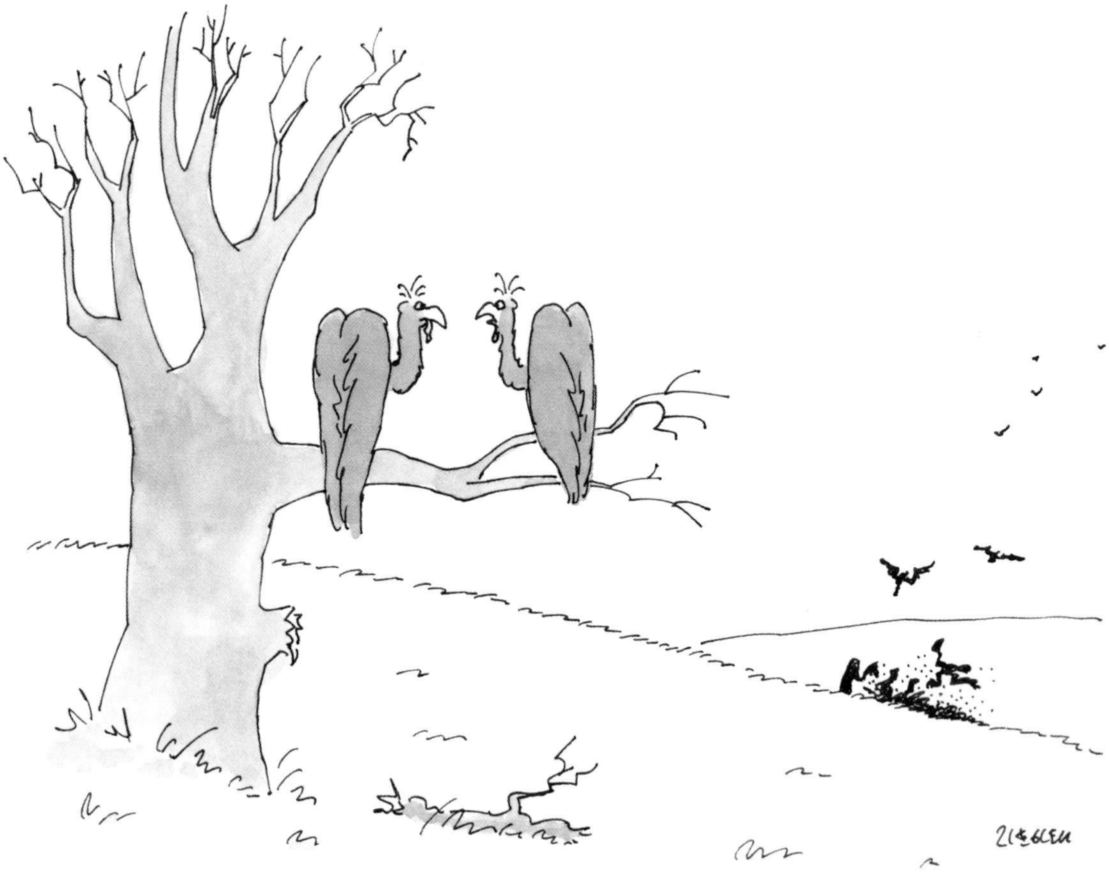
ZIEGLER

"You know what the Serengeti lacks? Decent desserts."

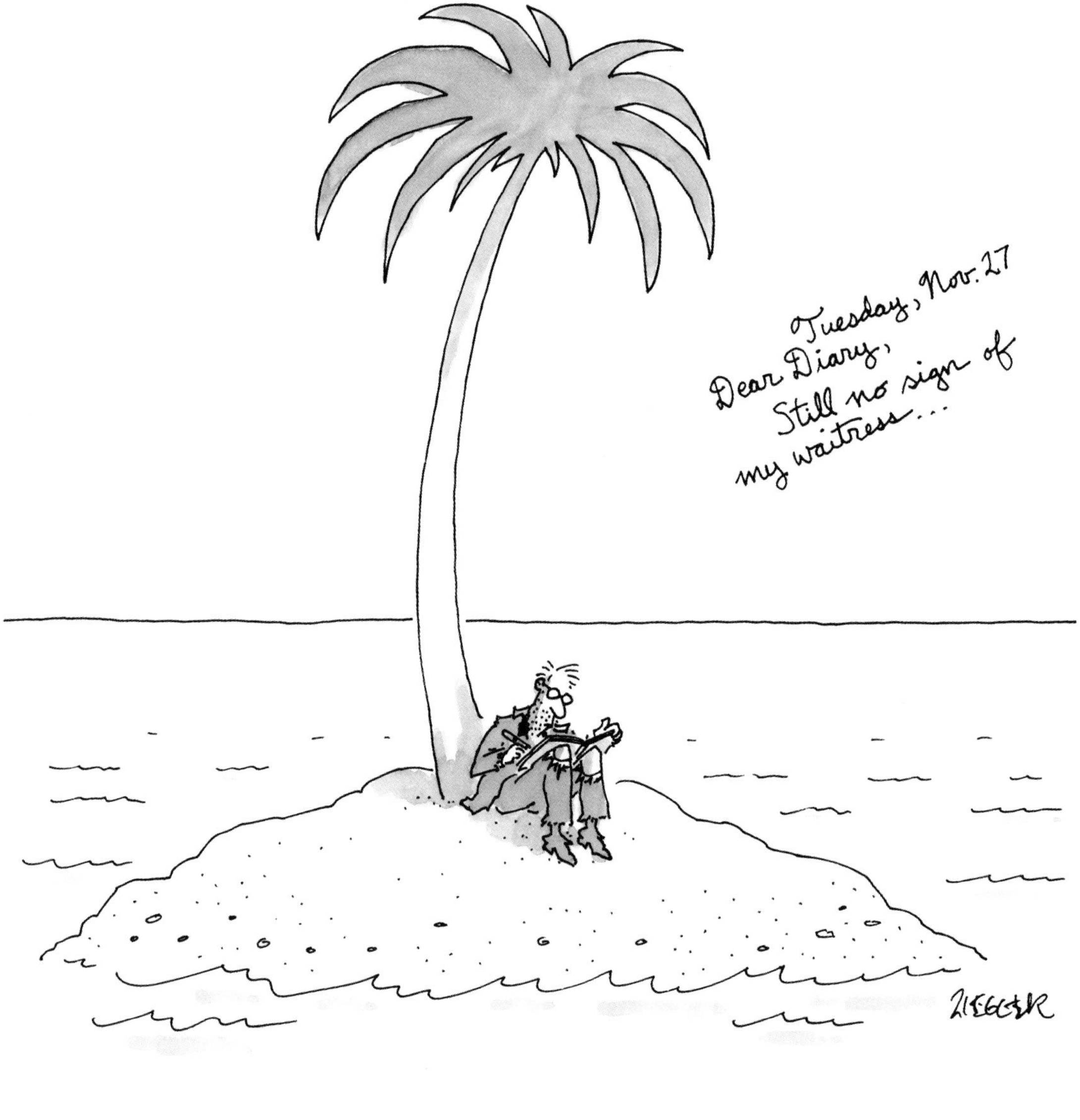
Tuesday, Nov. 27
Dear Diary,
Still no sign of
my waitress...
ZIEGLER

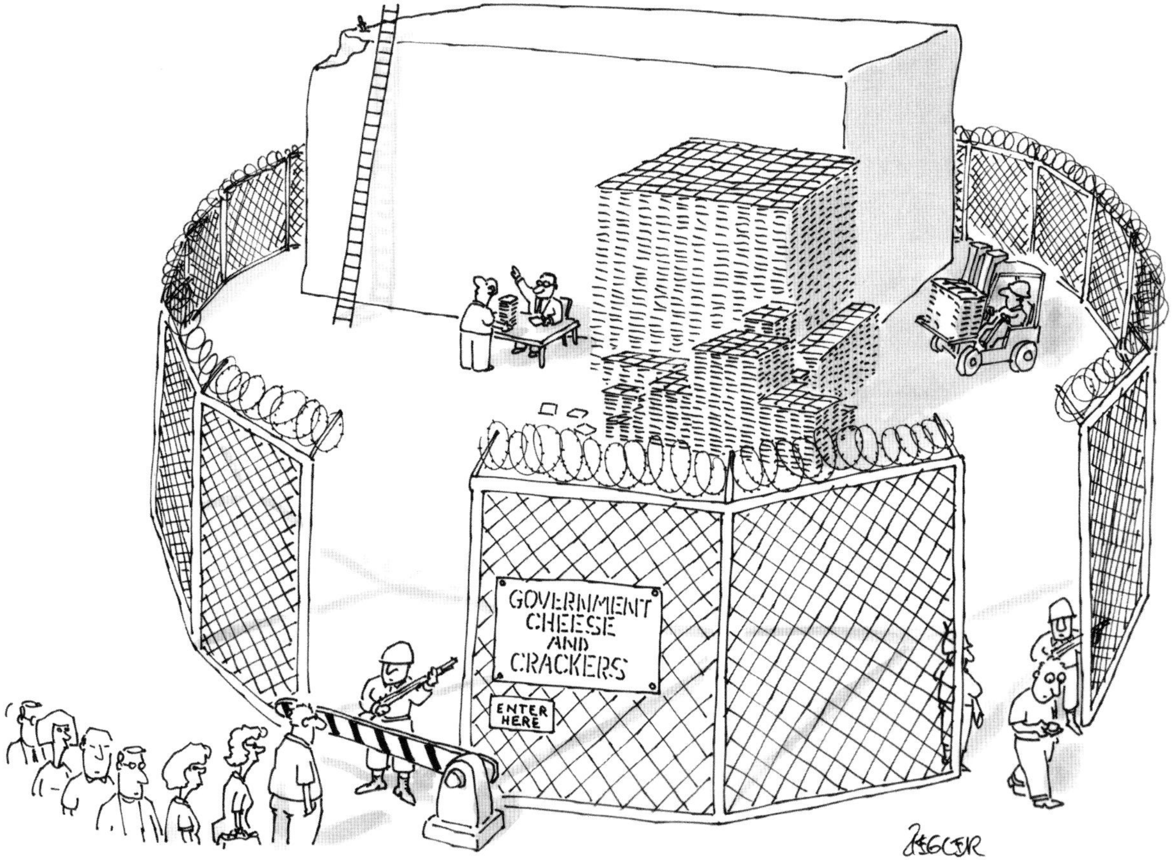
GOVERNMENT CHEESE AND CRACKERS
ENTER HERE

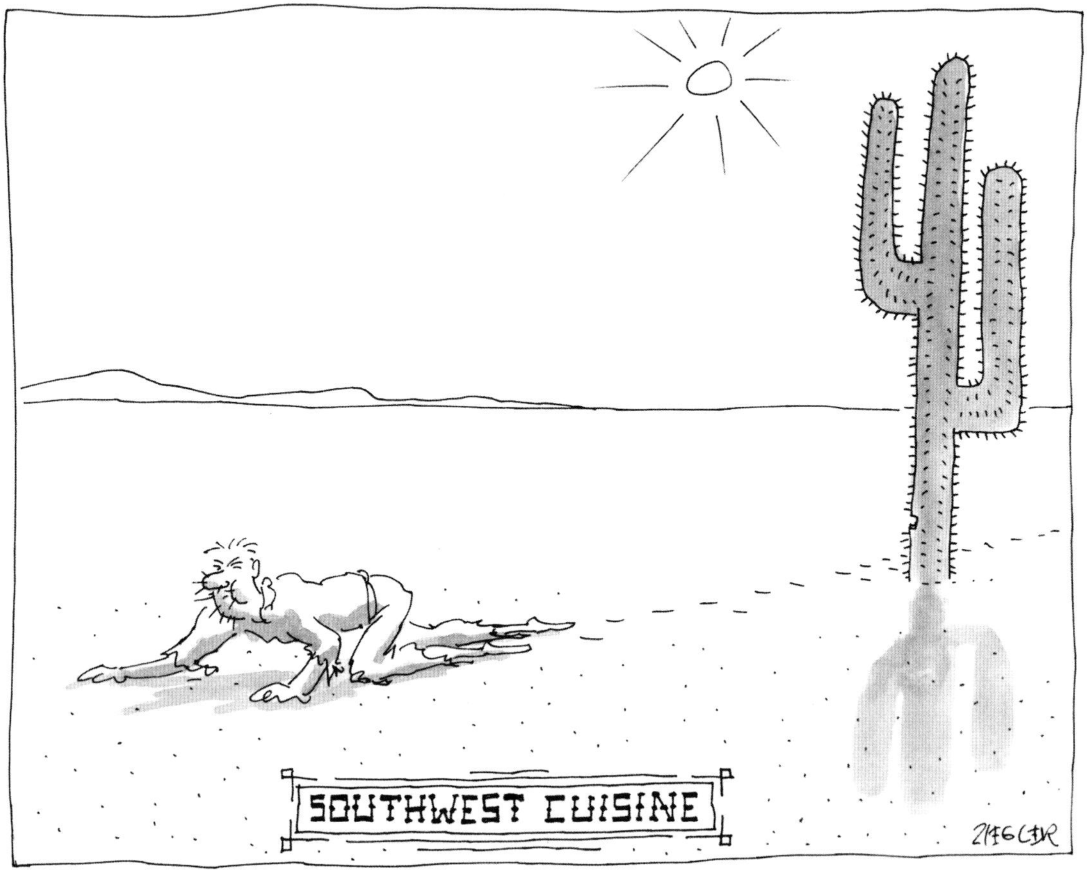
SOUTHWEST CUISINE
ZIEGLER

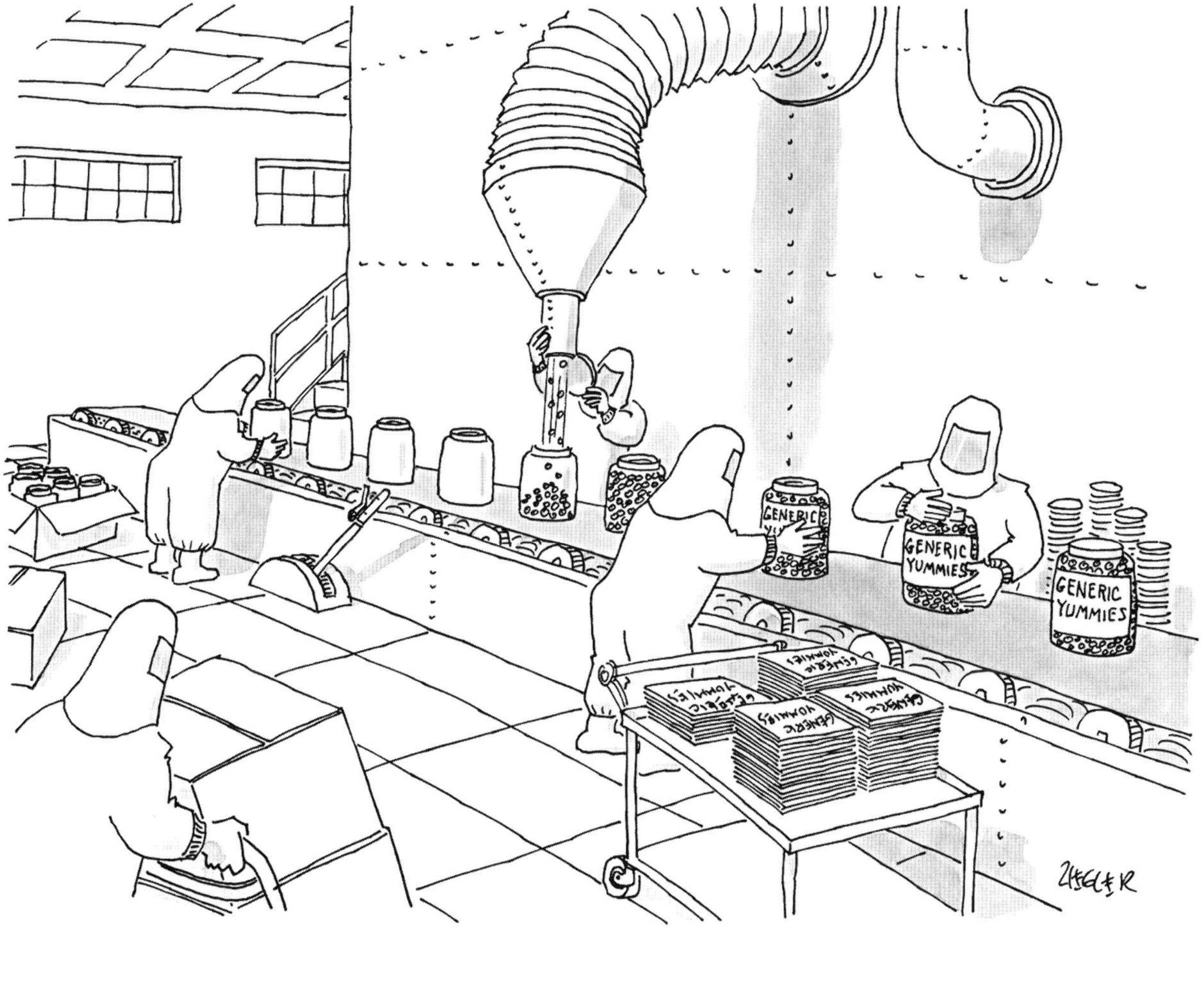
GENERIC YUMMIES
GENERIC YUMMIES
ZIEGLER

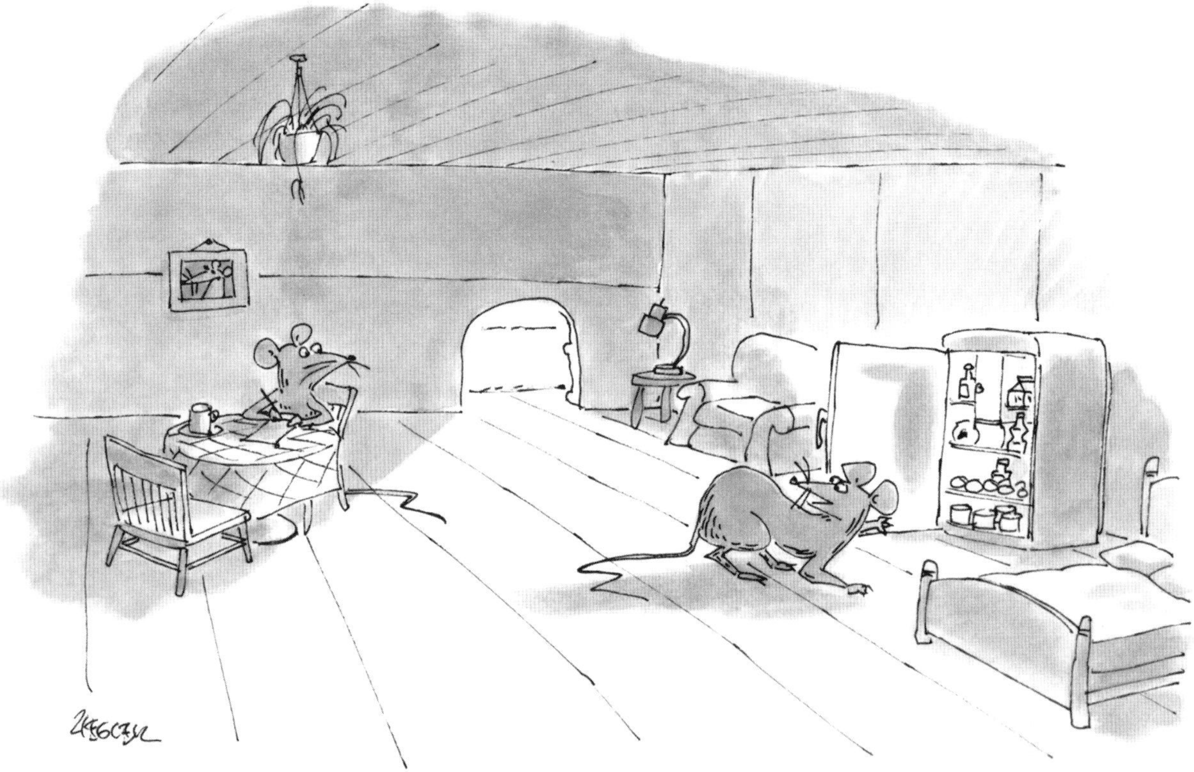
ZIEGLER

"We need milk, eggs, bread, cheese. Underline cheese."

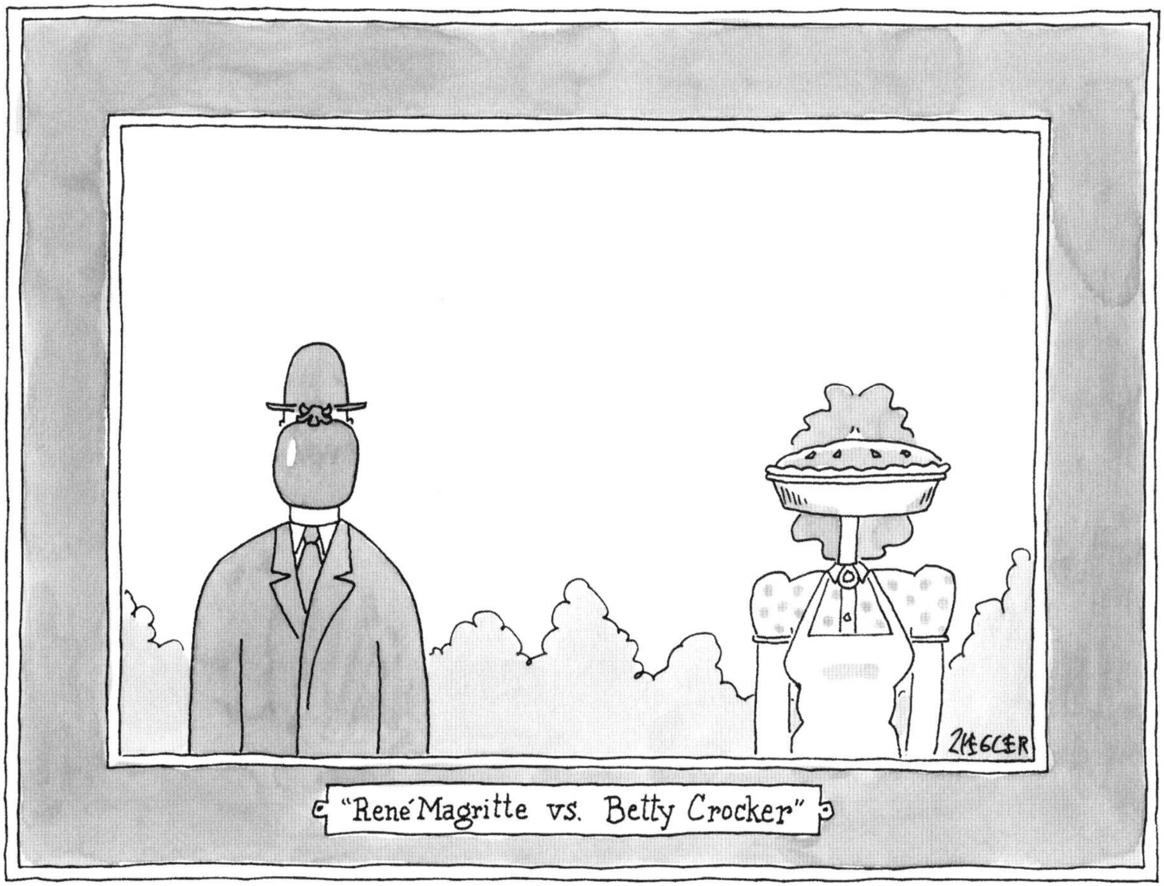
ZIEGLER
"René Magritte vs. Betty Crocker"

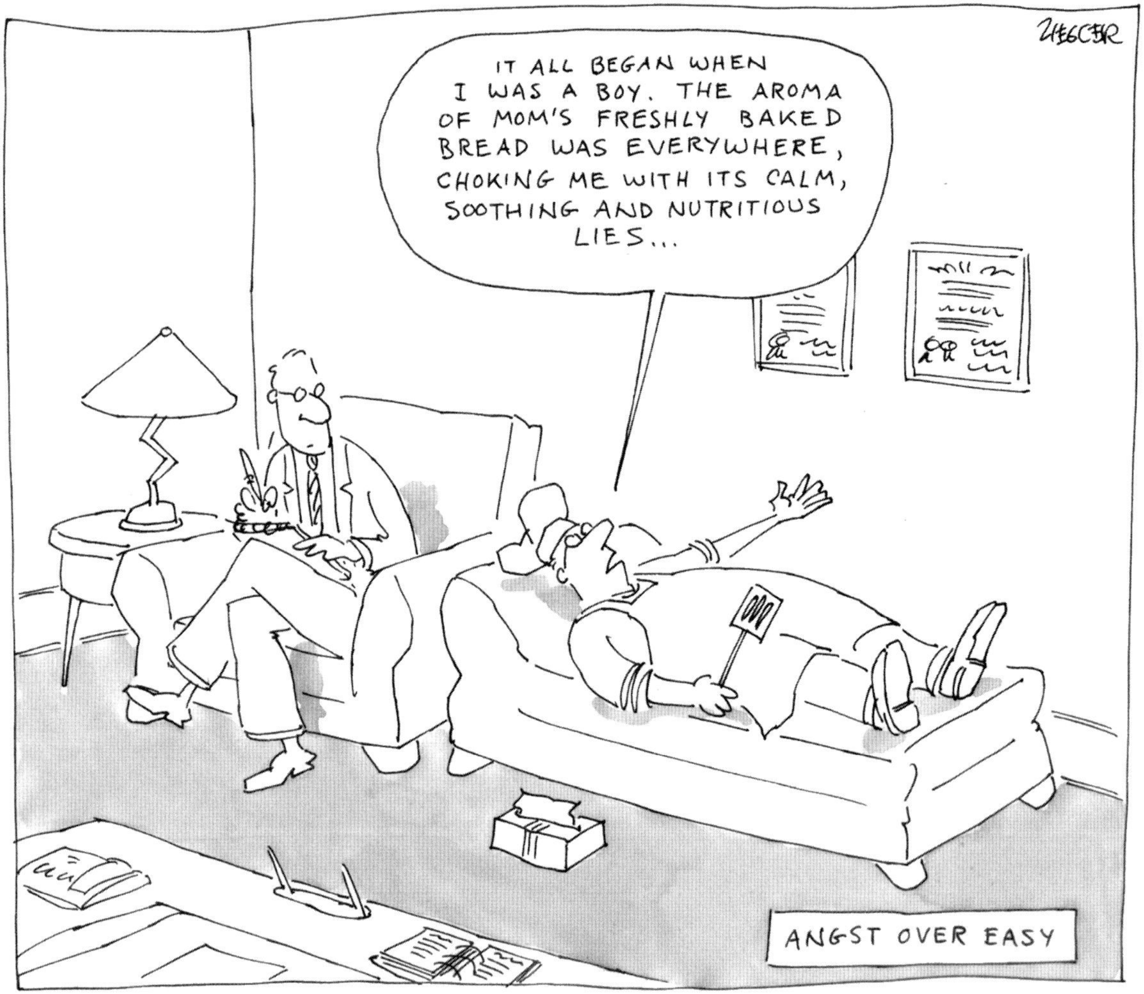
IT ALL BEGAN WHEN I WAS A BOY. THE AROMA OF MOM'S FRESHLY BAKED BREAD WAS EVERYWHERE, CHOKING ME WITH ITS CALM, SOOTHING AND NUTRITIOUS LIES...
ANGST OVER EASY

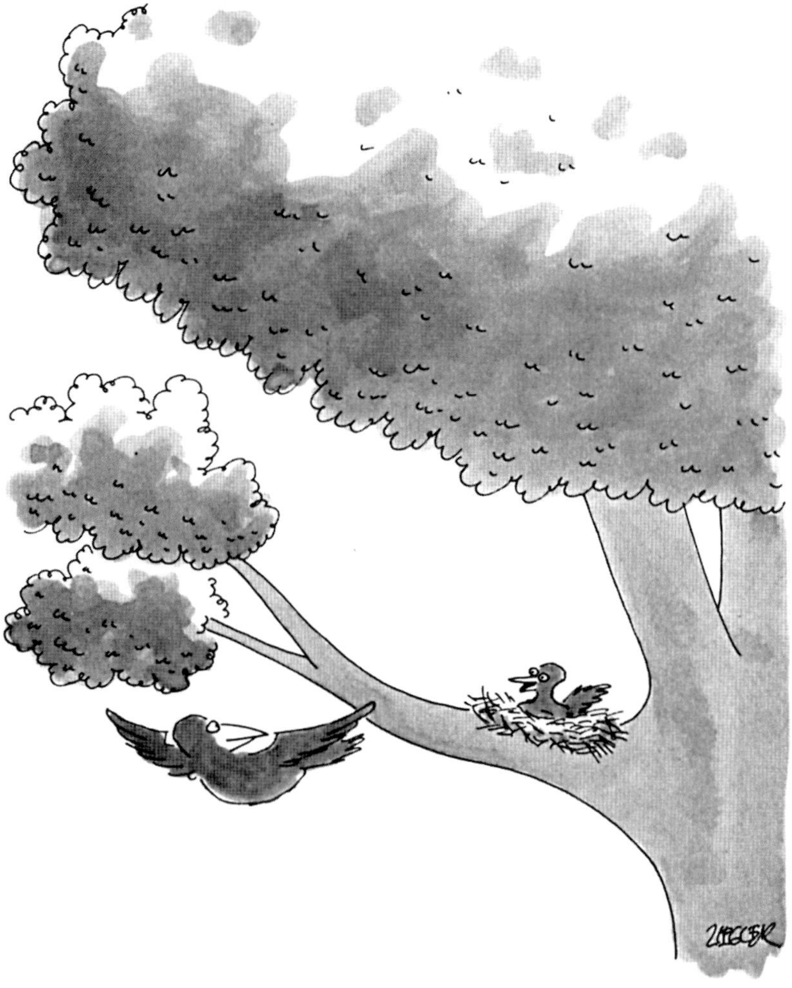
ZIEGLER

"Don't forget—grubs, mites, worms. I want this to be a very *special evening."*

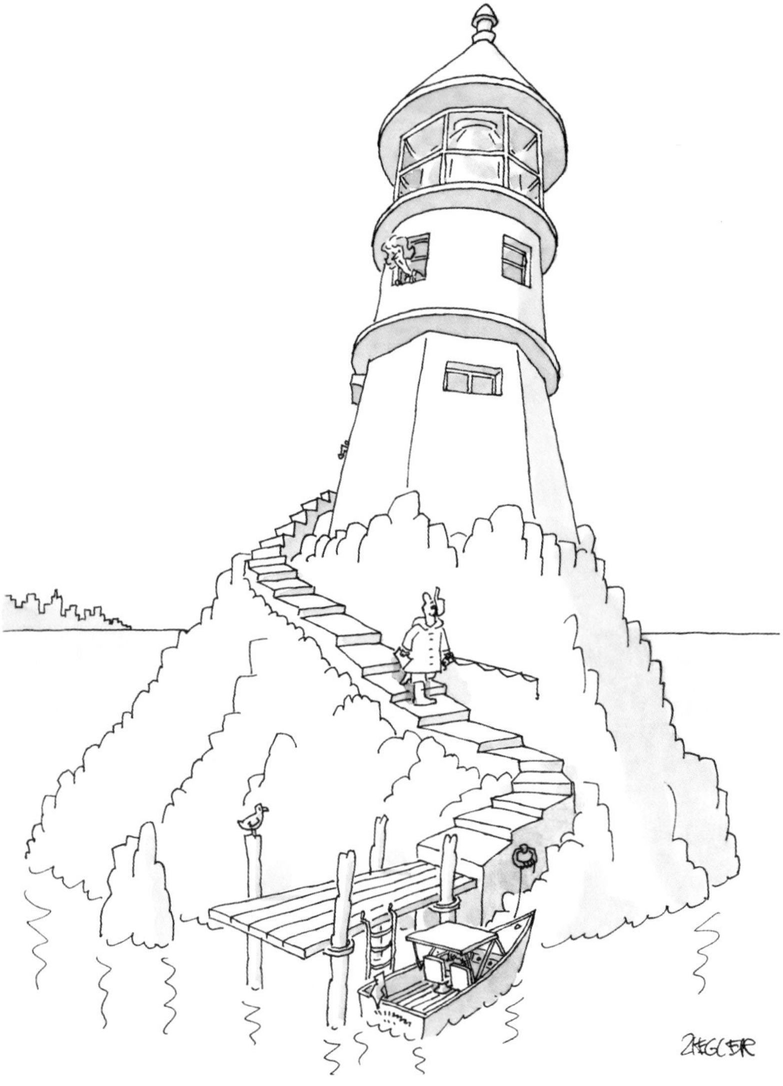
ZIEGLER

"And pick up a wine—something that goes with fish."

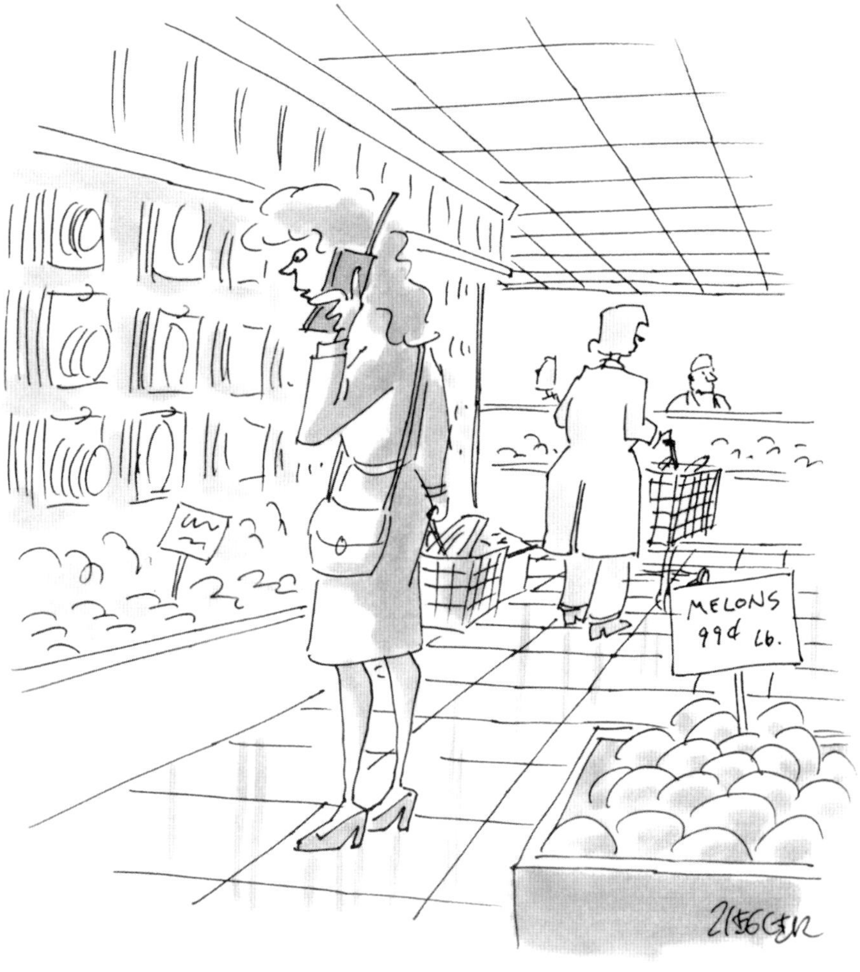
MELONS
99¢ Lb.

"Oscar Meyar or Hormel?"

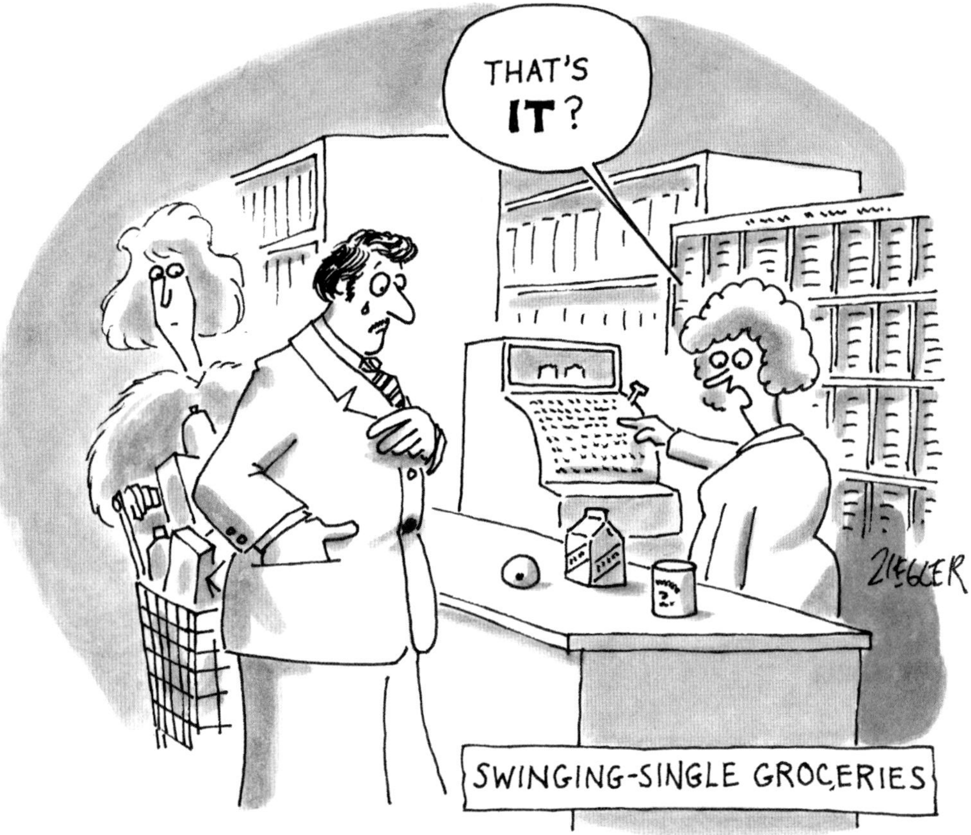
THAT'S
IT?
SWINGING-SINGLE GROCERIES
ZIEGLER

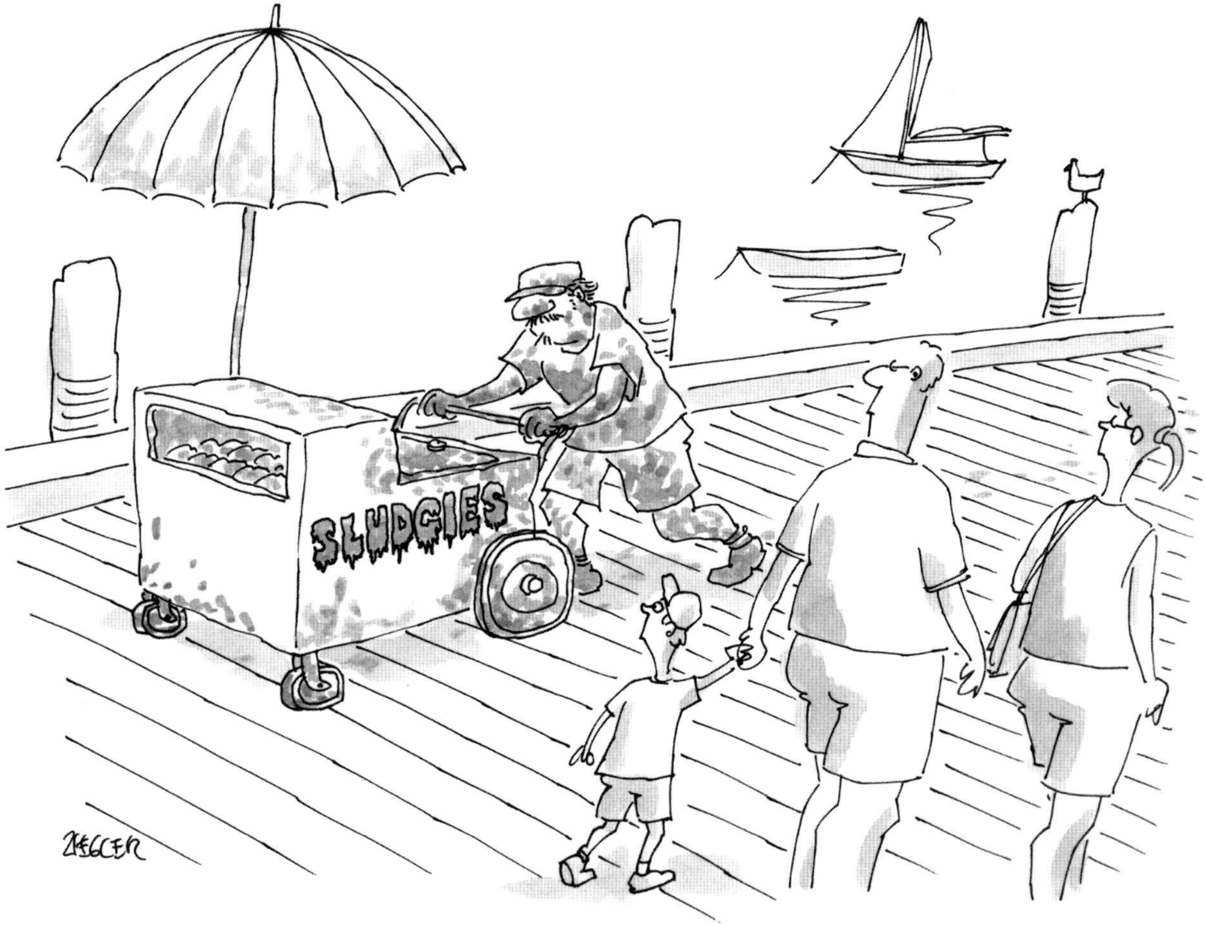
SLUDGIES
ZIEGLER

METRO GOLDWYN MACARONI

ZIEGLER

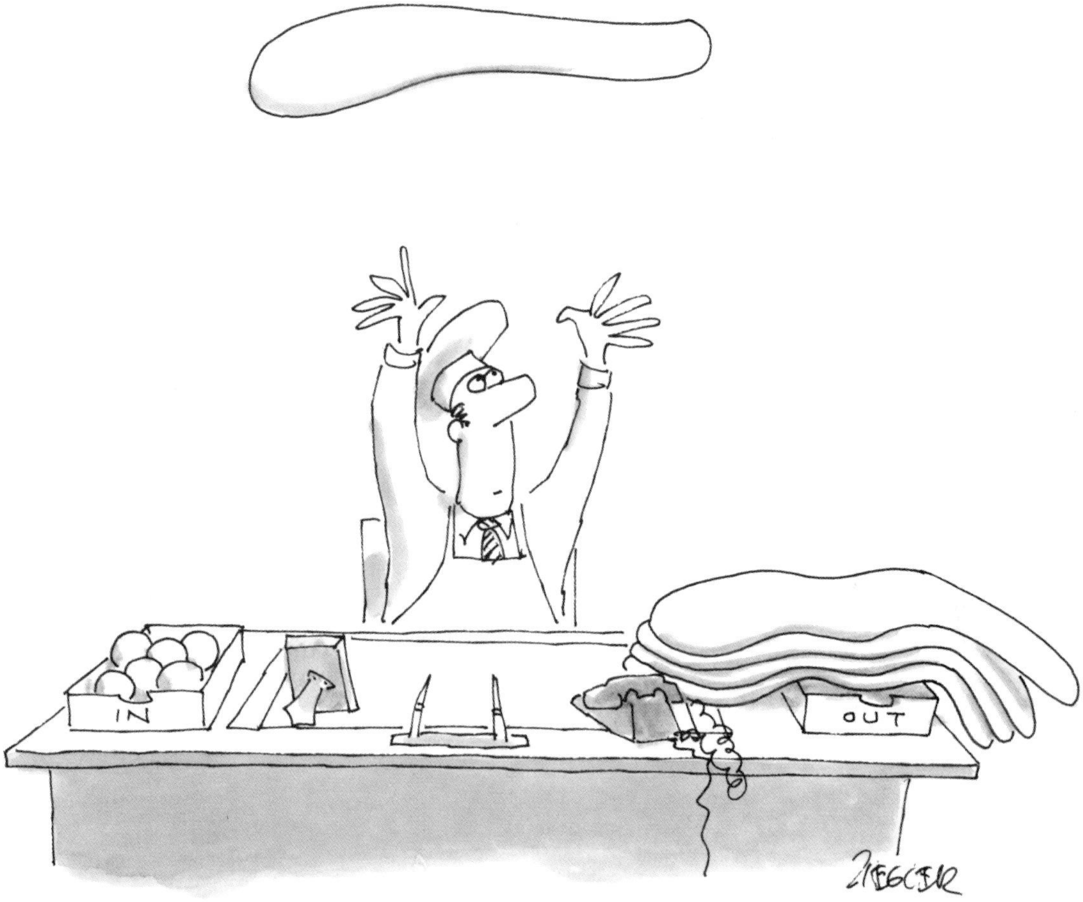
IN
OUT
ZIEGLER

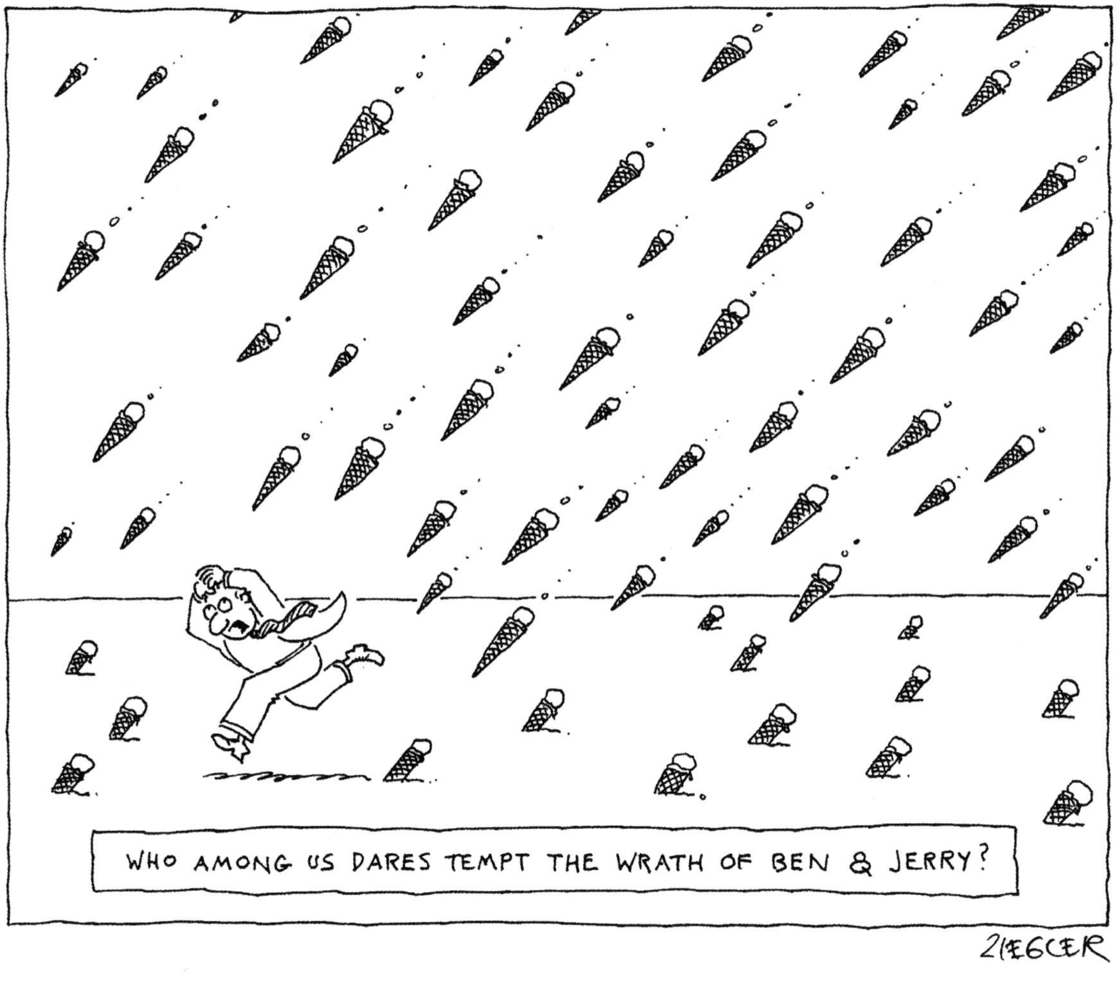
WHO AMONG US DARES TEMPT THE WRATH OF BEN & JERRY?
ZIEGLER

THE WONDERFUL WORLD OF CHEESE
CHEESE BOARD
CHEESE KNOB
CHEESE CUTTER
CHEESE CRACKERS
CHEESE WEDGE
CHEESE LEFTOVERS
ZIEGLER

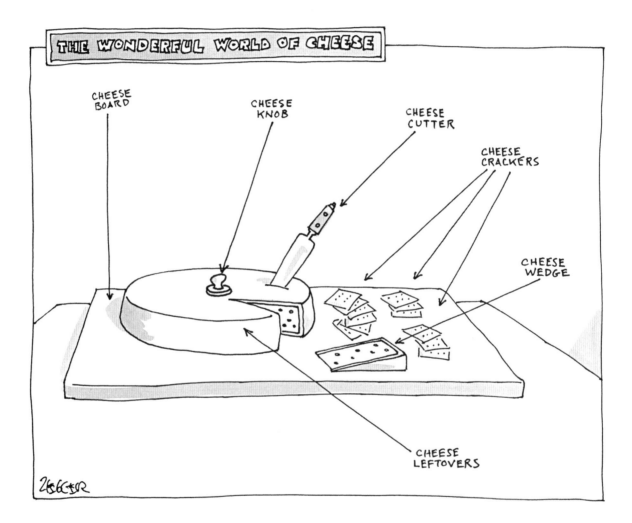

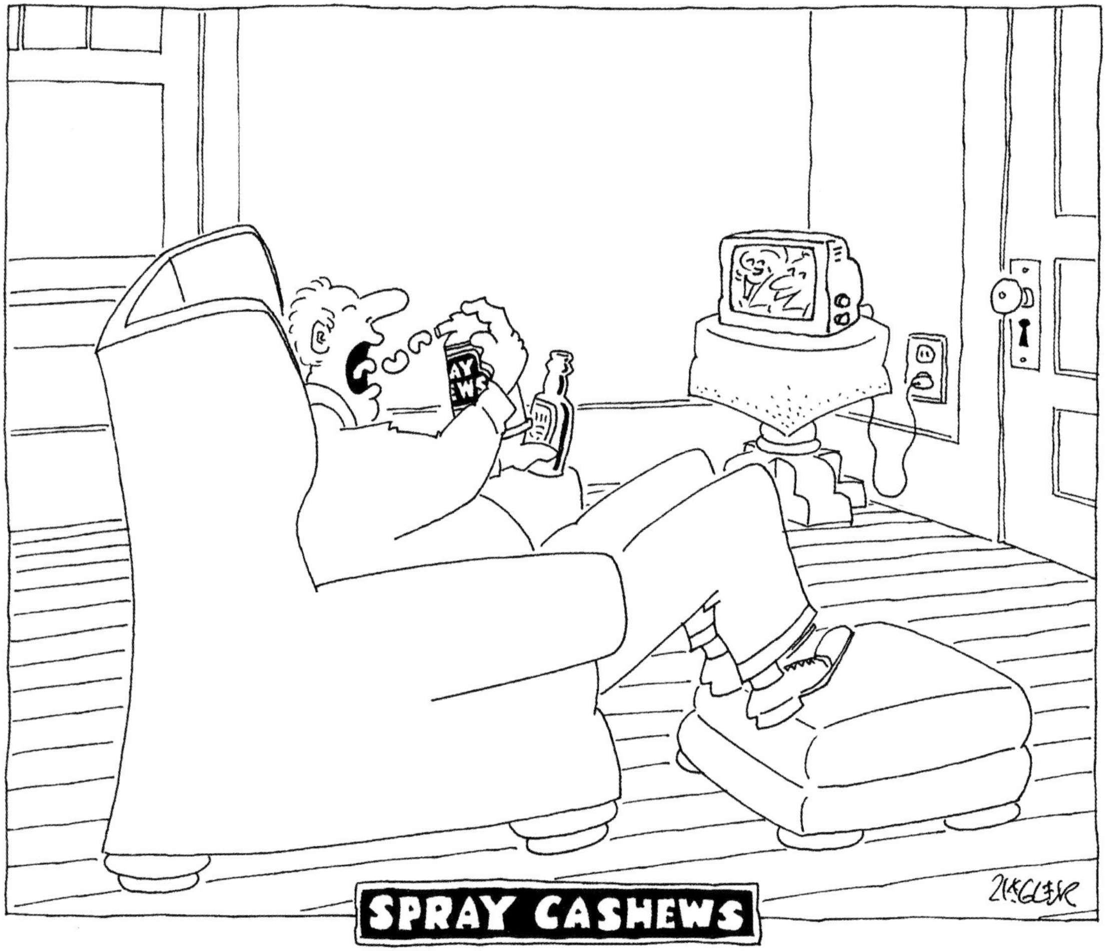
SPRAY CASHEWS
ZIEGLER

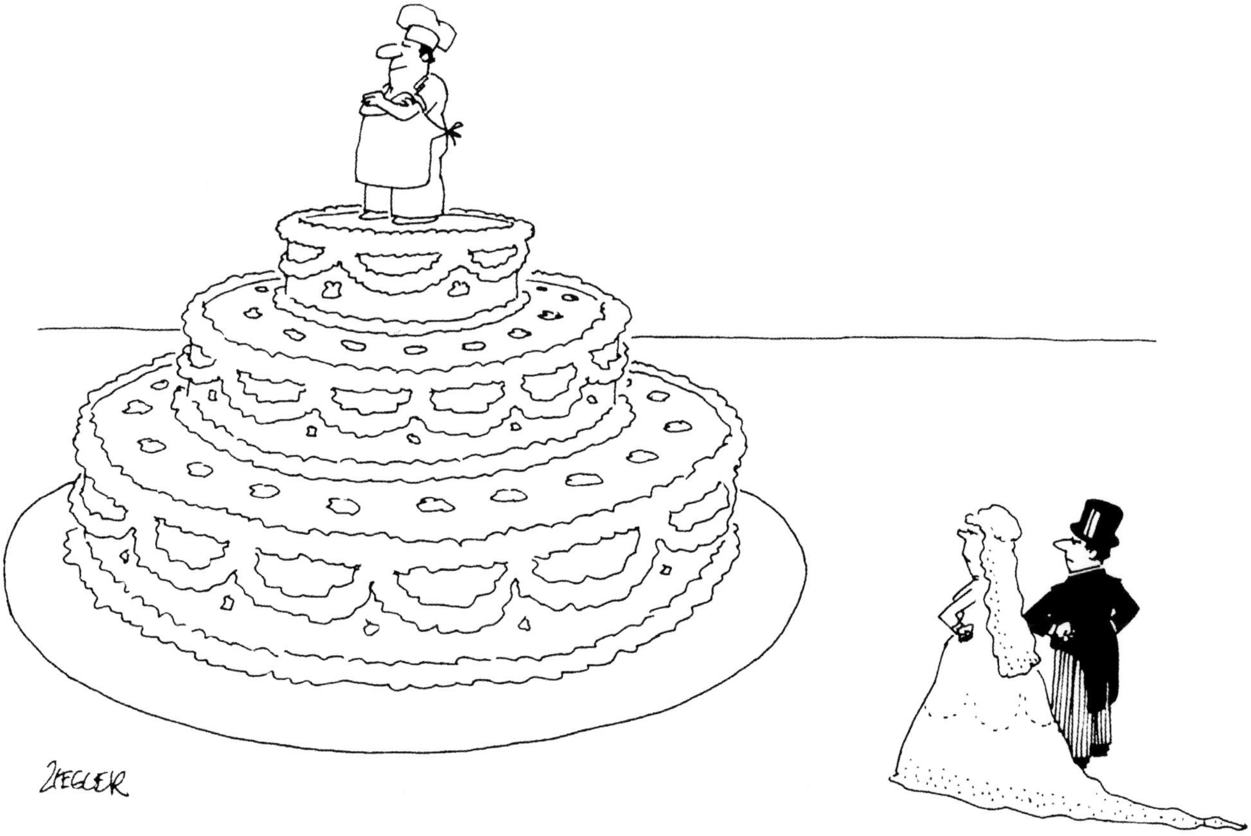
ZIEGLER

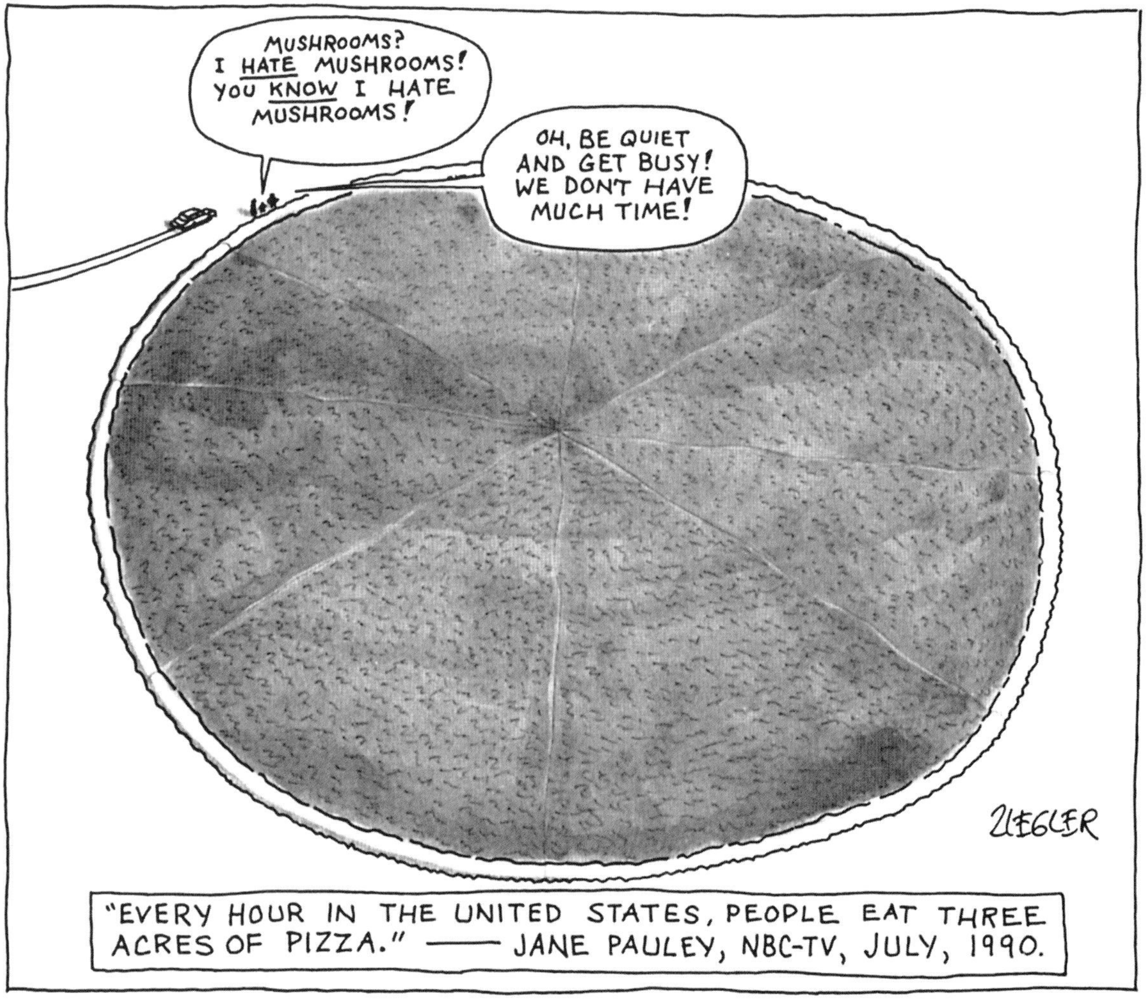
MUSHROOMS? I HATE MUSHROOMS! YOU KNOW I HATE MUSHROOMS!
OH, BE QUIET AND GET BUSY! WE DON'T HAVE MUCH TIME!
ZIEGLER

"EVERY HOUR IN THE UNITED STATES, PEOPLE EAT THREE ACRES OF PIZZA." —— JANE PAULEY, NBC-TV, JULY, 1990.

"Most would order red, but I prefer a fine, dry white with my jerky."

LO-CAL BAR SNAX

MEATLESS BUFFALO WINGS

SALTED BEV NAPS

OYSTER LICK

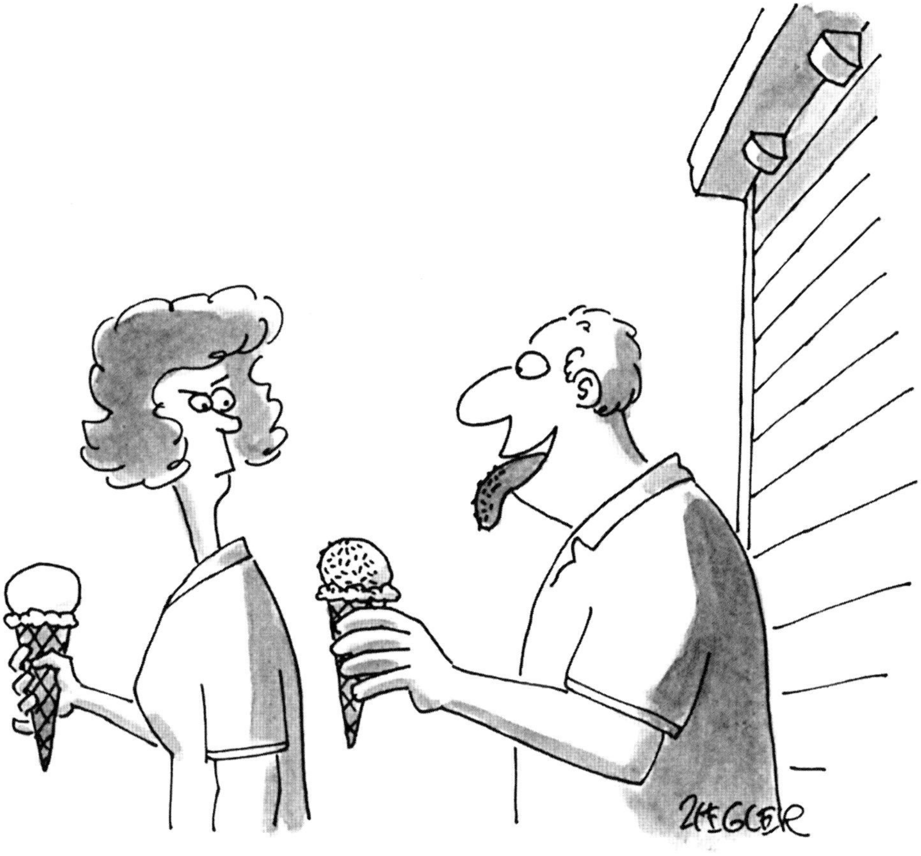
ZIEGLER

"Thprinklth."

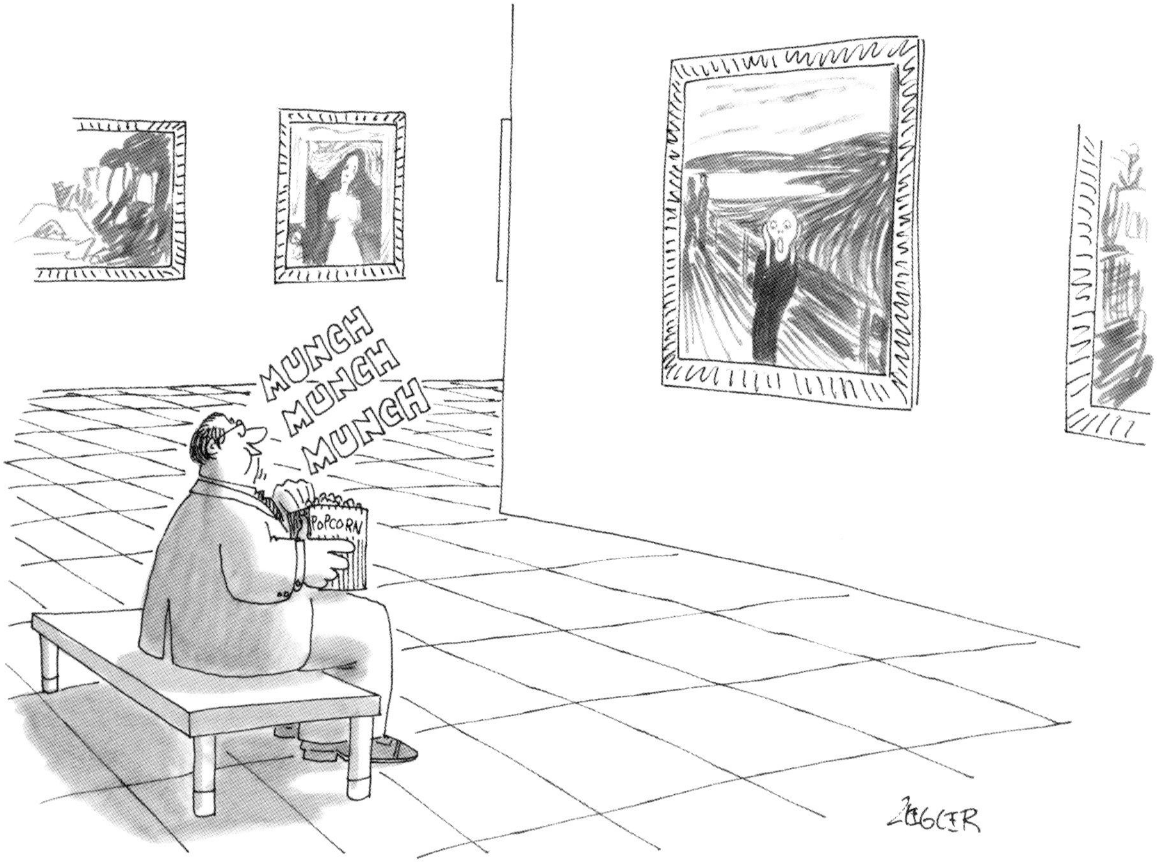
MUNCH
MUNCH
MUNCH
POPCORN
ZIEGLER

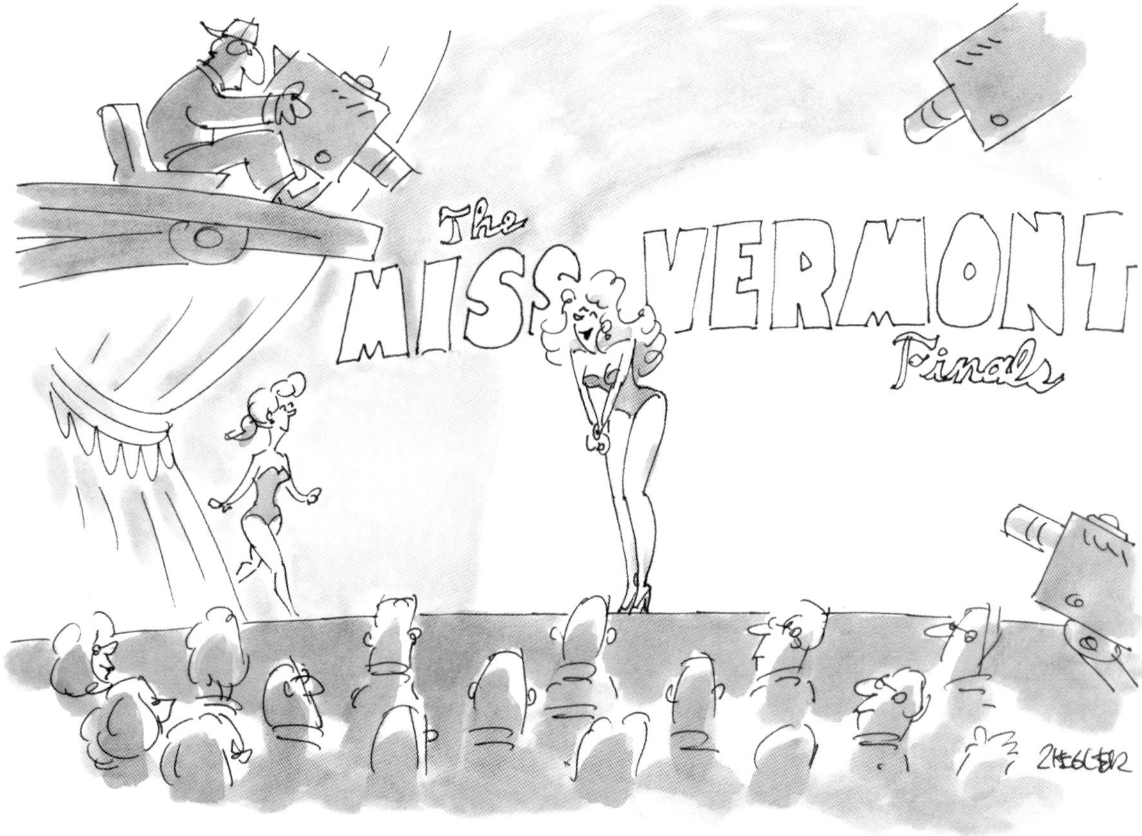
The
MISS VERMONT
Finals

"Hi. My name is Tanya and, if elected, my agenda will be cheddar! Cheddar, cheddar, cheddar!!"

BUDGET MUNCHIES

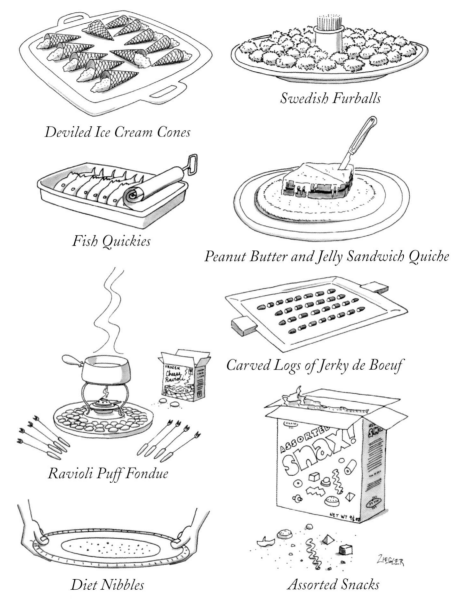

Deviled Ice Cream Cones

Swedish Furballs

Fish Quickies

Peanut Butter and Jelly Sandwich Quiche

FROZEN
Cheese Ravioli

Ravioli Puff Fondue

Carved Logs of Jerky de Boeuf

Diet Nibbles

ASSORTED
snax!
ZIEGLER

Assorted Snacks

"O.K. are we ready? Good! Chef George, go plug in the neon 'Eat' sign."

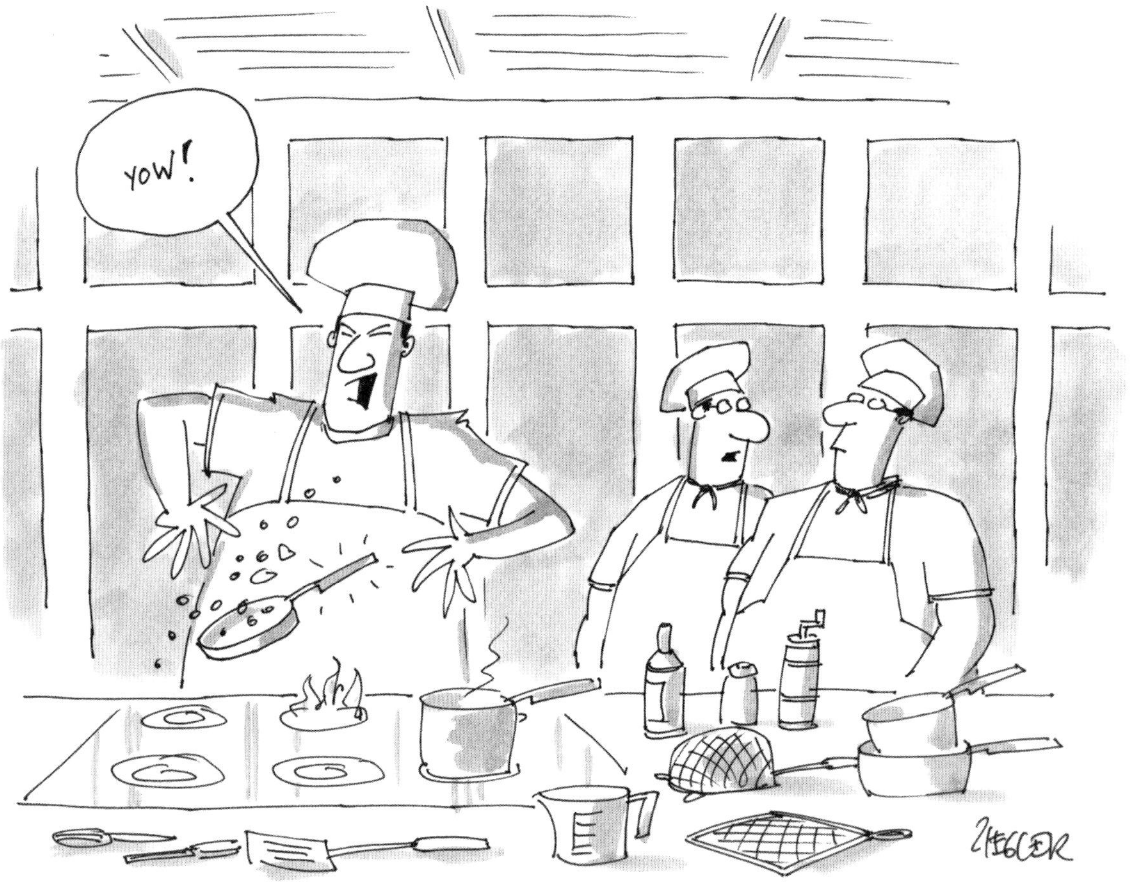
YOW!

"Iron Chef, my ass!"

"*Mmm. The soup du jour is not cream of mushroom. It is not tomato or celery. It is not chicken, nor is it Scotch broth. It is most definitely not won ton. . . .*"

THE SUPER JUMBO EXTRA LARGE WITH NOTHING ON IT

"It's only the Ericksons, so why don't you just use the recalled hamburger meat."

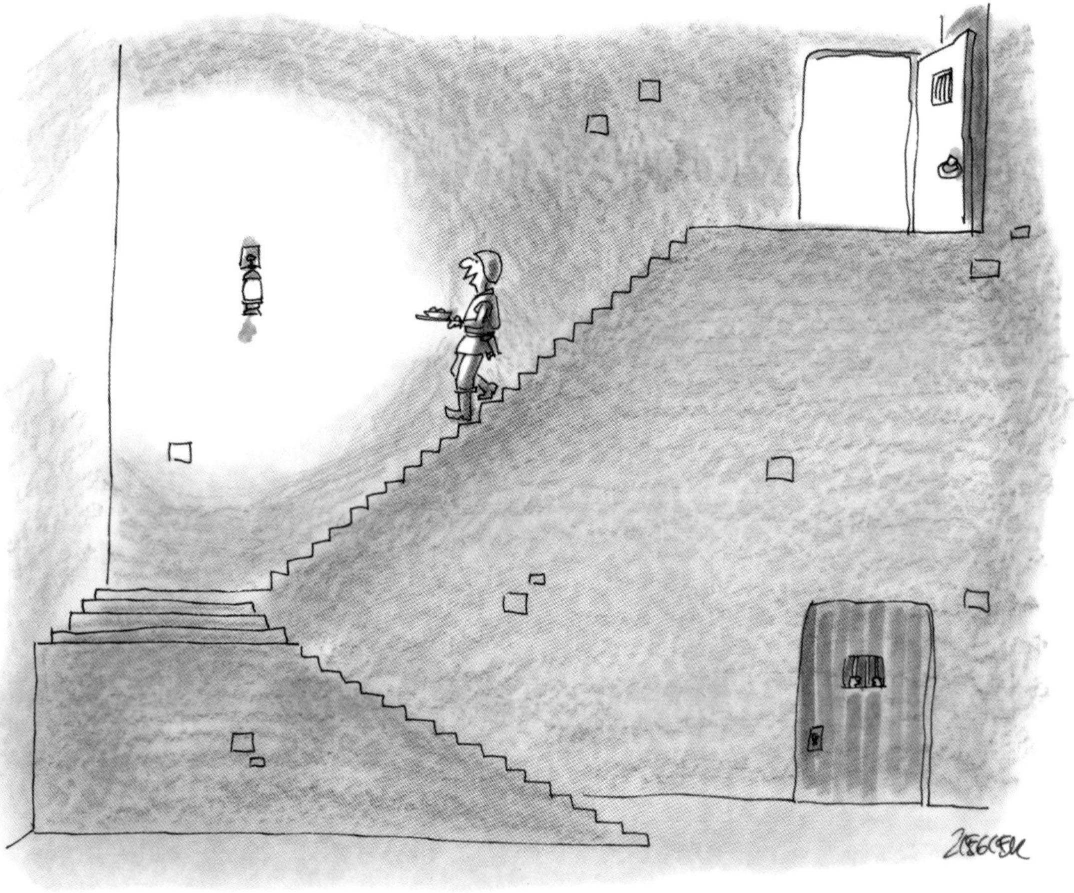
ZIEGLER

"Come and get it! Ha, ha—just kidding."

"Tonight—just for a change—let's see if we can get through dinner without eating anything at all."

"*Would the gentleman care for a razor and comb to start?*"

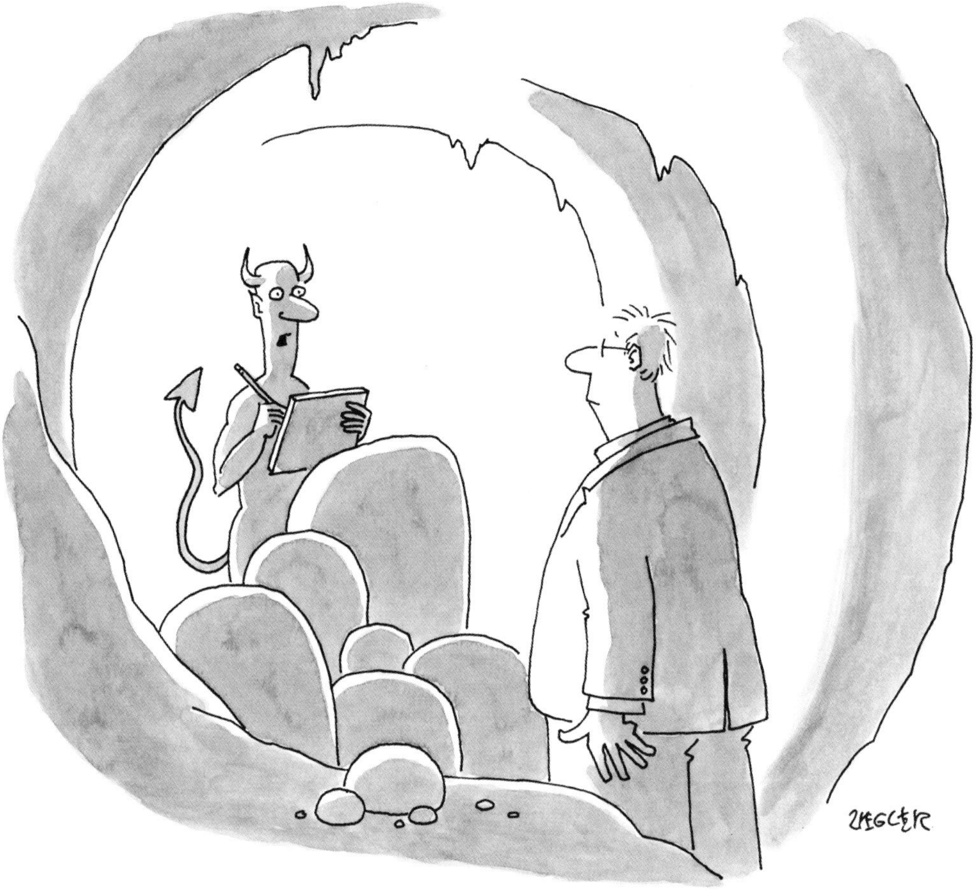
ZIEGLER

"And lastly, for all eternity, French, blue cheese, or ranch?"

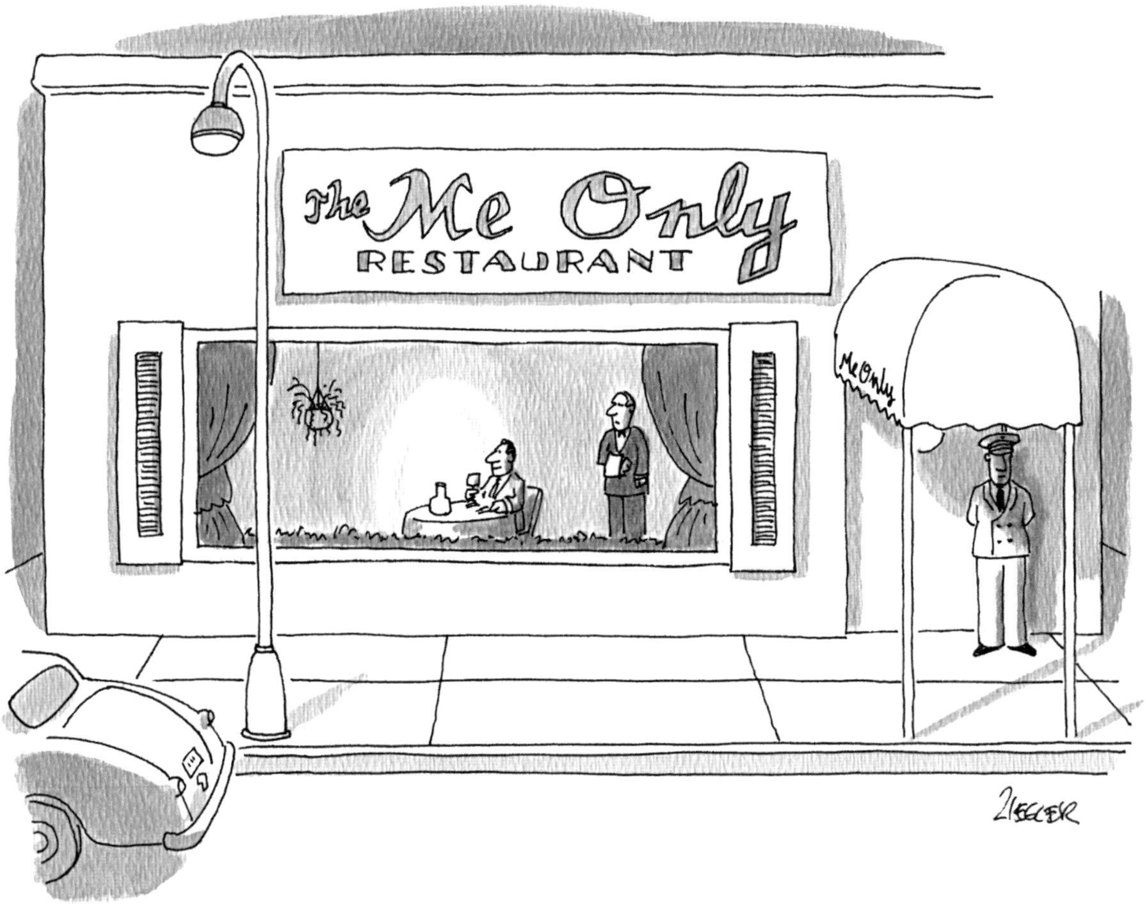
The Me Only
RESTAURANT
Me Only
ZIEGLER

"We'll start with the appetizer, move on to the entree, and then finish up with dessert."

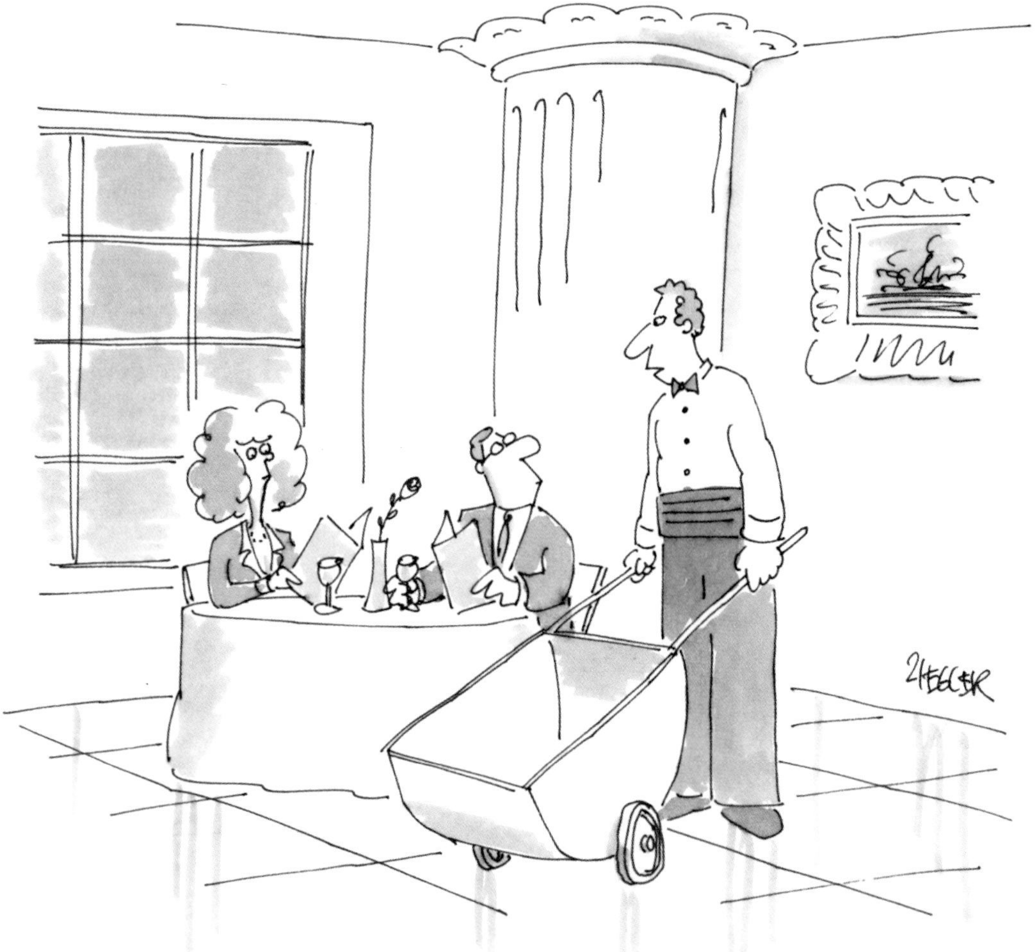
ZIEGLER

"Are you folks familiar with our portions?"

"Cat Yummies again?"

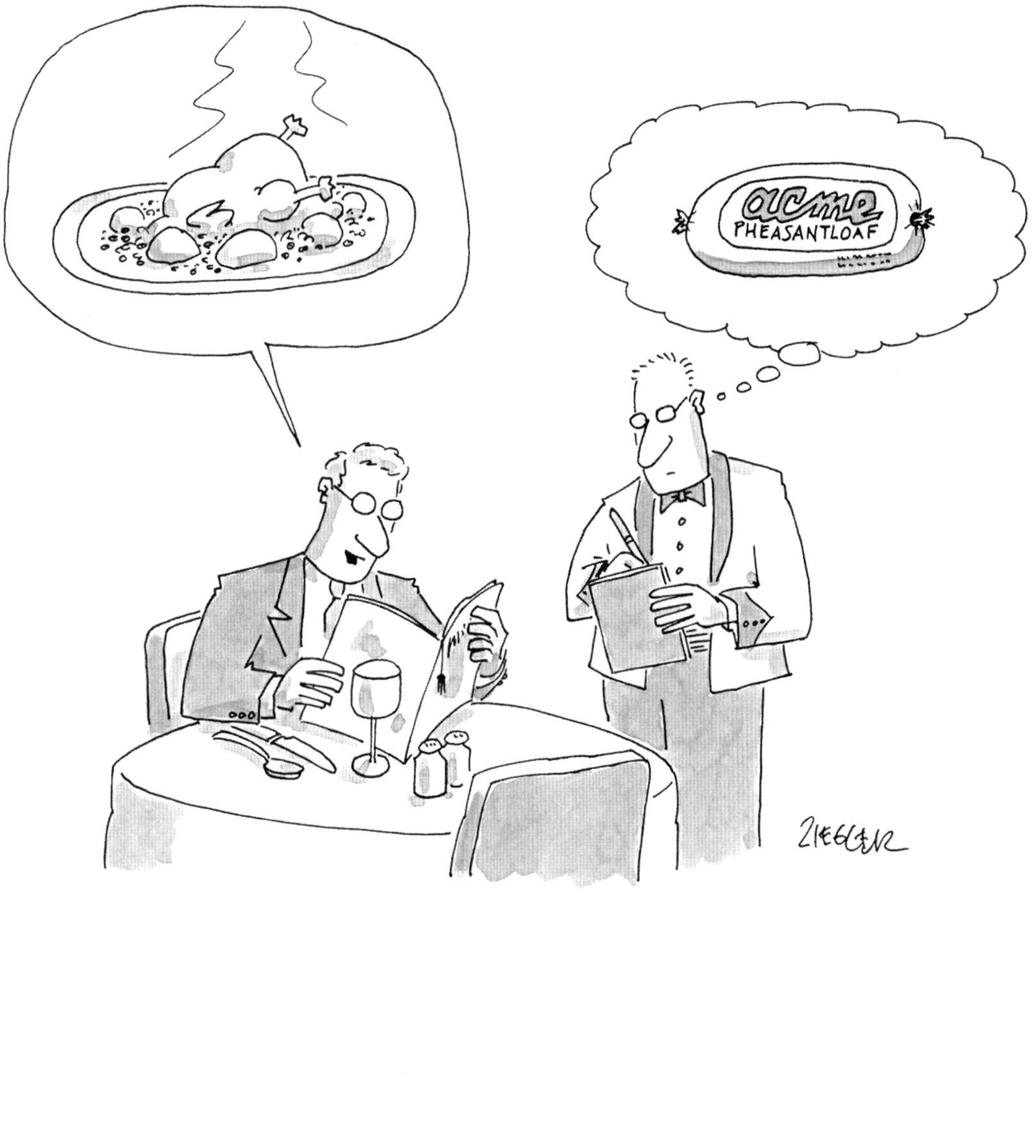
acme
PHEASANTLOAF
ZIEGLER

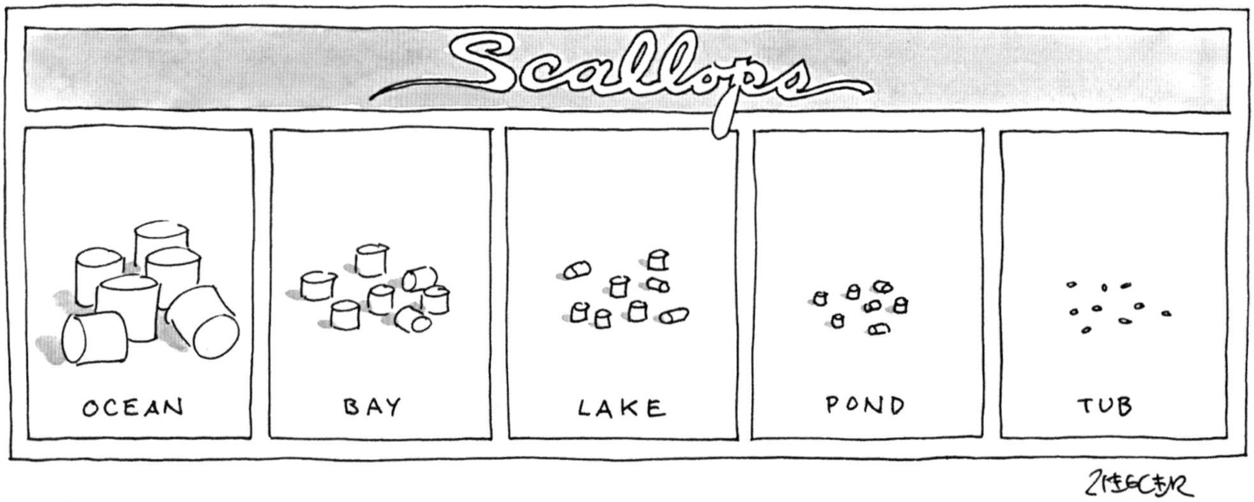
Scallops
OCEAN
BAY
LAKE
POND
TUB

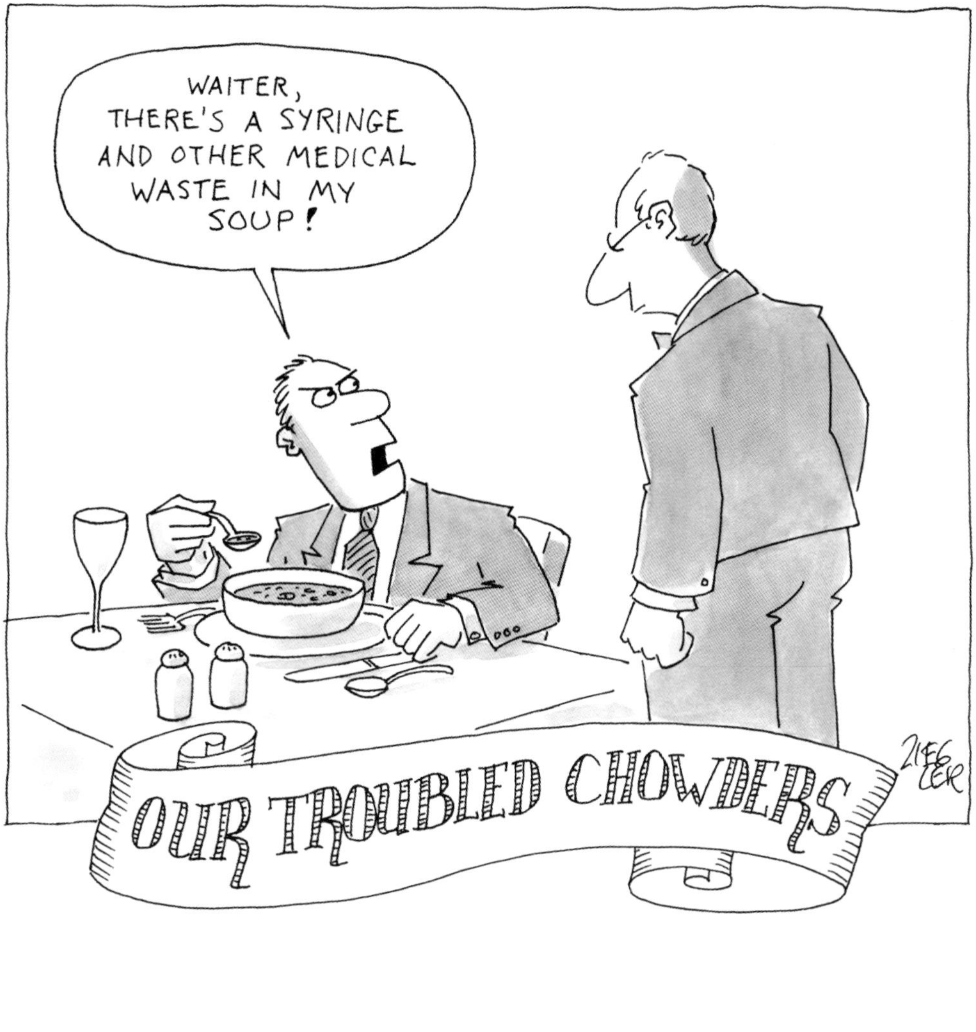
WAITER, THERE'S A SYRINGE AND OTHER MEDICAL WASTE IN MY SOUP!
OUR TROUBLED CHOWDERS
ZIEGLER

"Is there any ketchup in the house?"

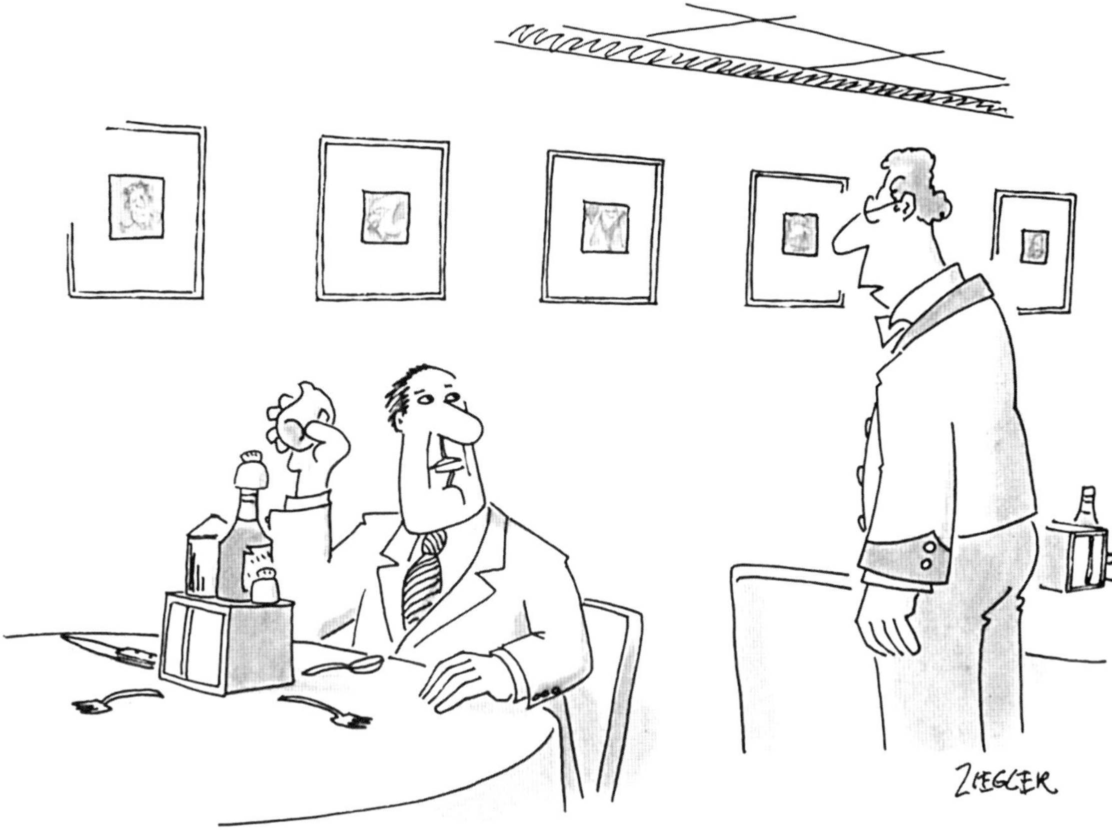
ZIEGLER

"When you've concluded the entertainment portion of your evening, sir, I'll be happy to bring you your entree."

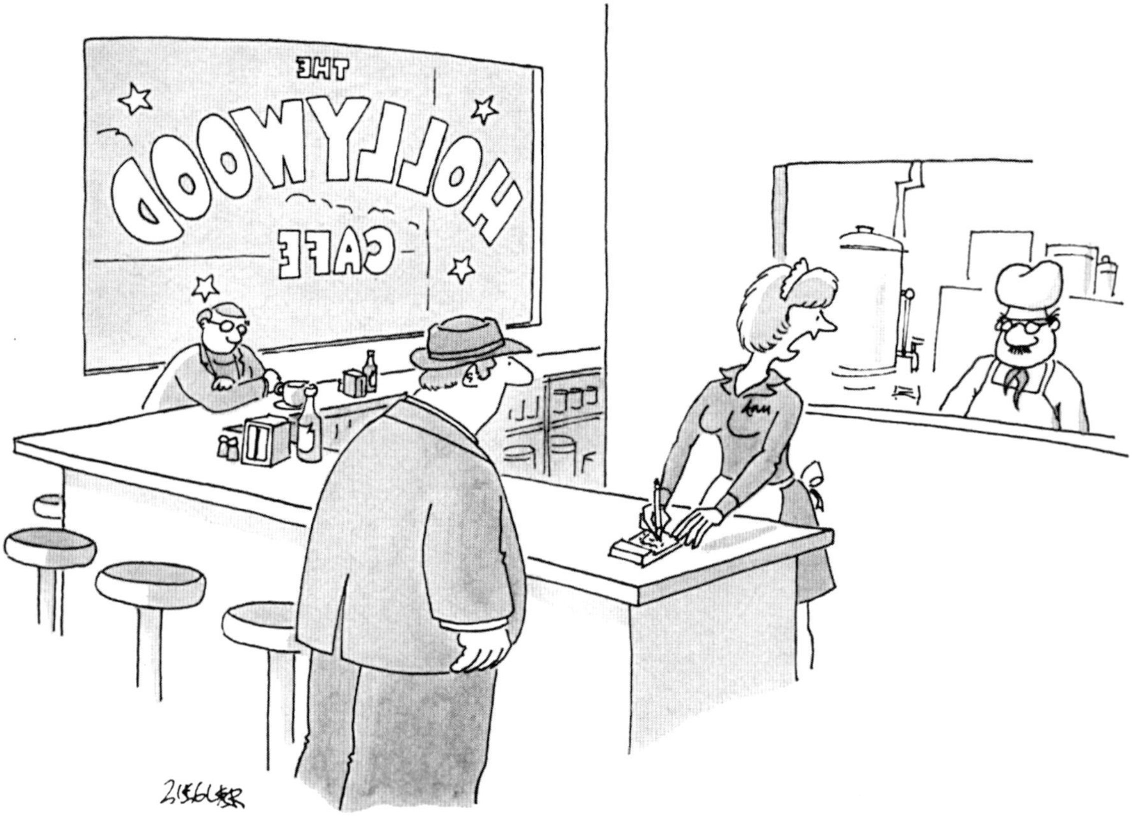
THE
HOLLYWOOD
CAFE

"Two Cagneys and a side of Garbo to go. Hold the Bogart."

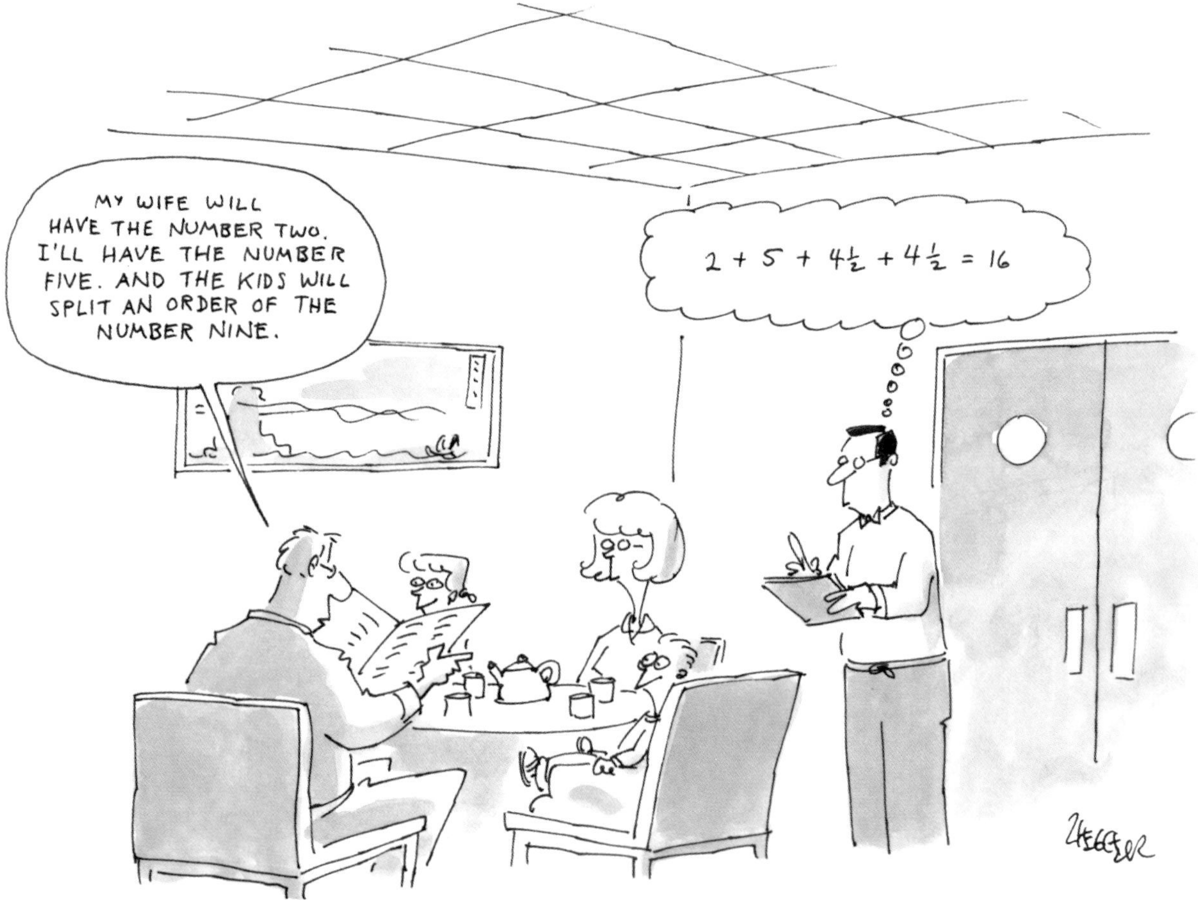
MY WIFE WILL HAVE THE NUMBER TWO. I'LL HAVE THE NUMBER FIVE. AND THE KIDS WILL SPLIT AN ORDER OF THE NUMBER NINE.
2 + 5 + 4½ + 4½ = 16

"*I know what you're thinking. You're thinking, 'Hey, what is this crap?'*"

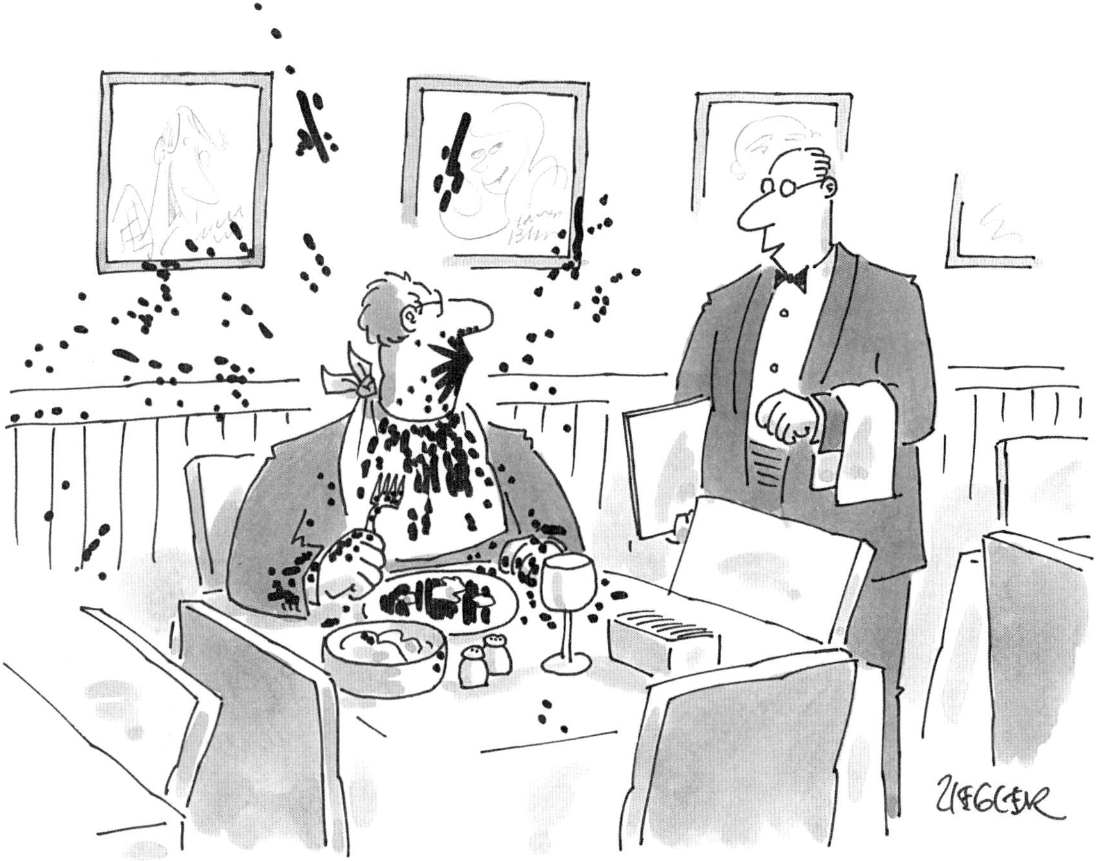
ZIEGLER

"How's the squid?"

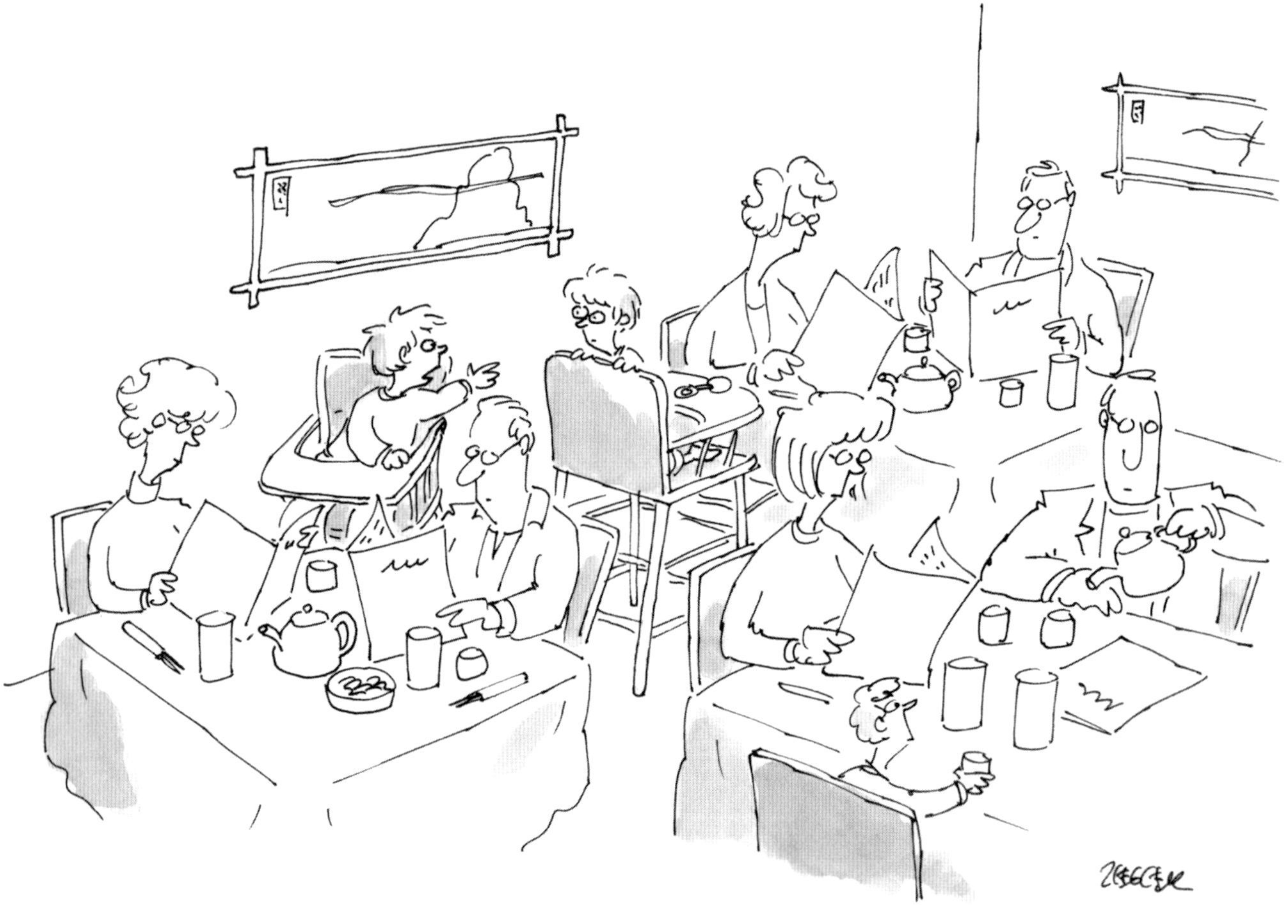

"I've had the bean curd lo mein, the kung po gai ding, and the fortune cookie and, believe me, hands down, the fortune cookie wins every time."

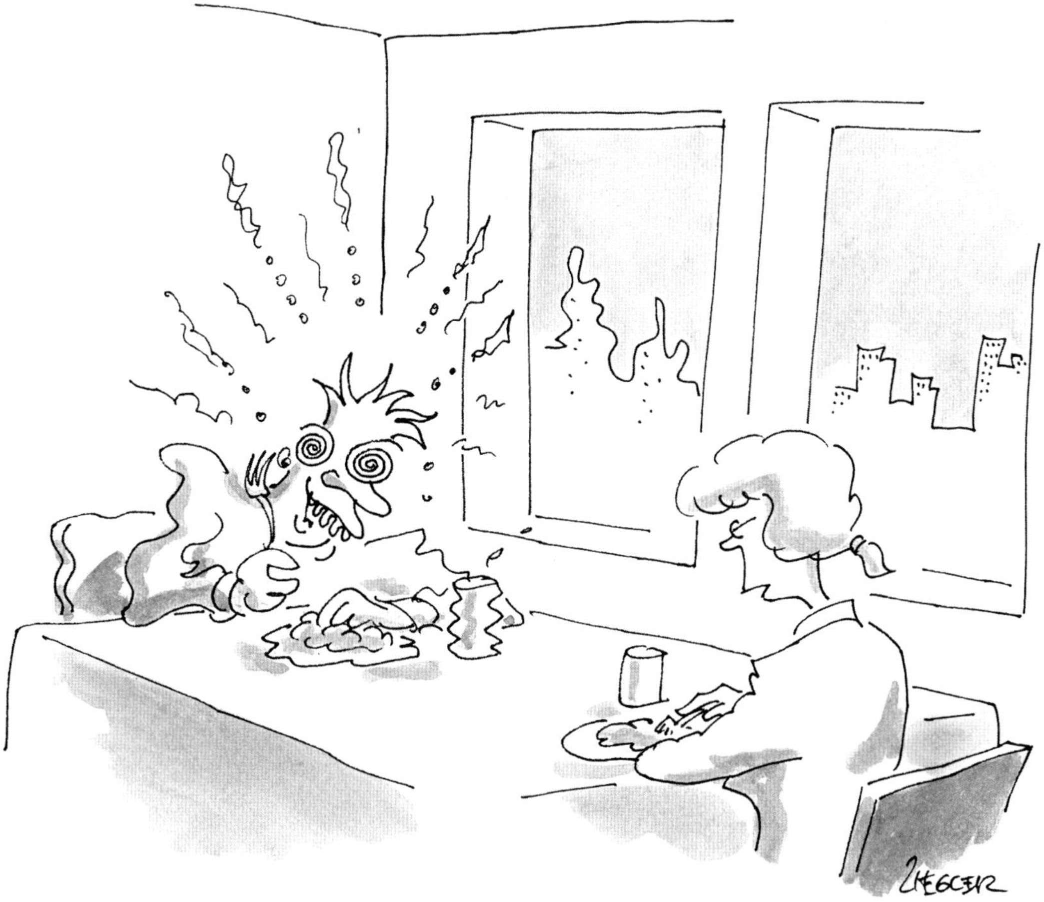
ZIEGLER

"Ken Kesey left us the recipe in his will."

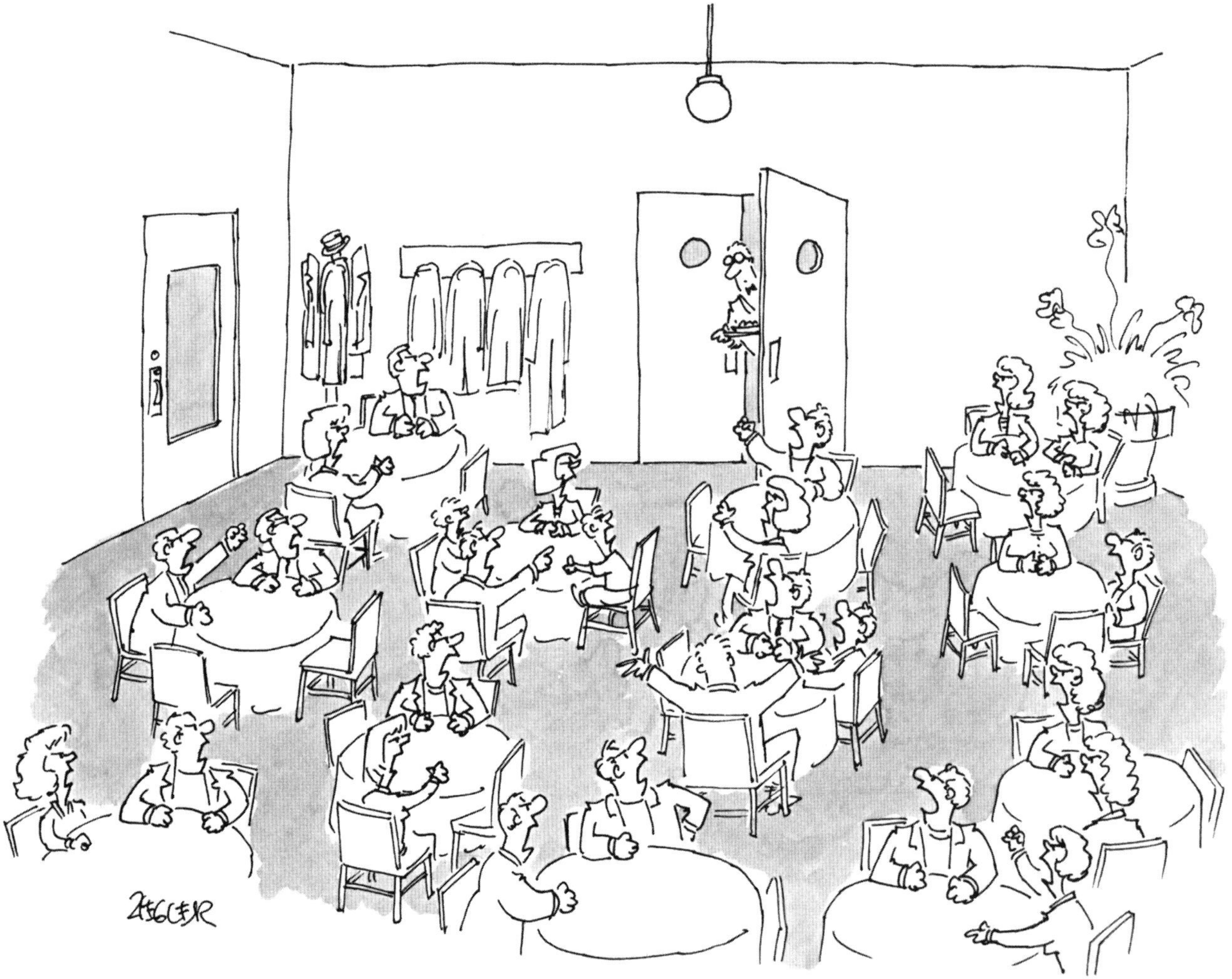

"Well, finally!"

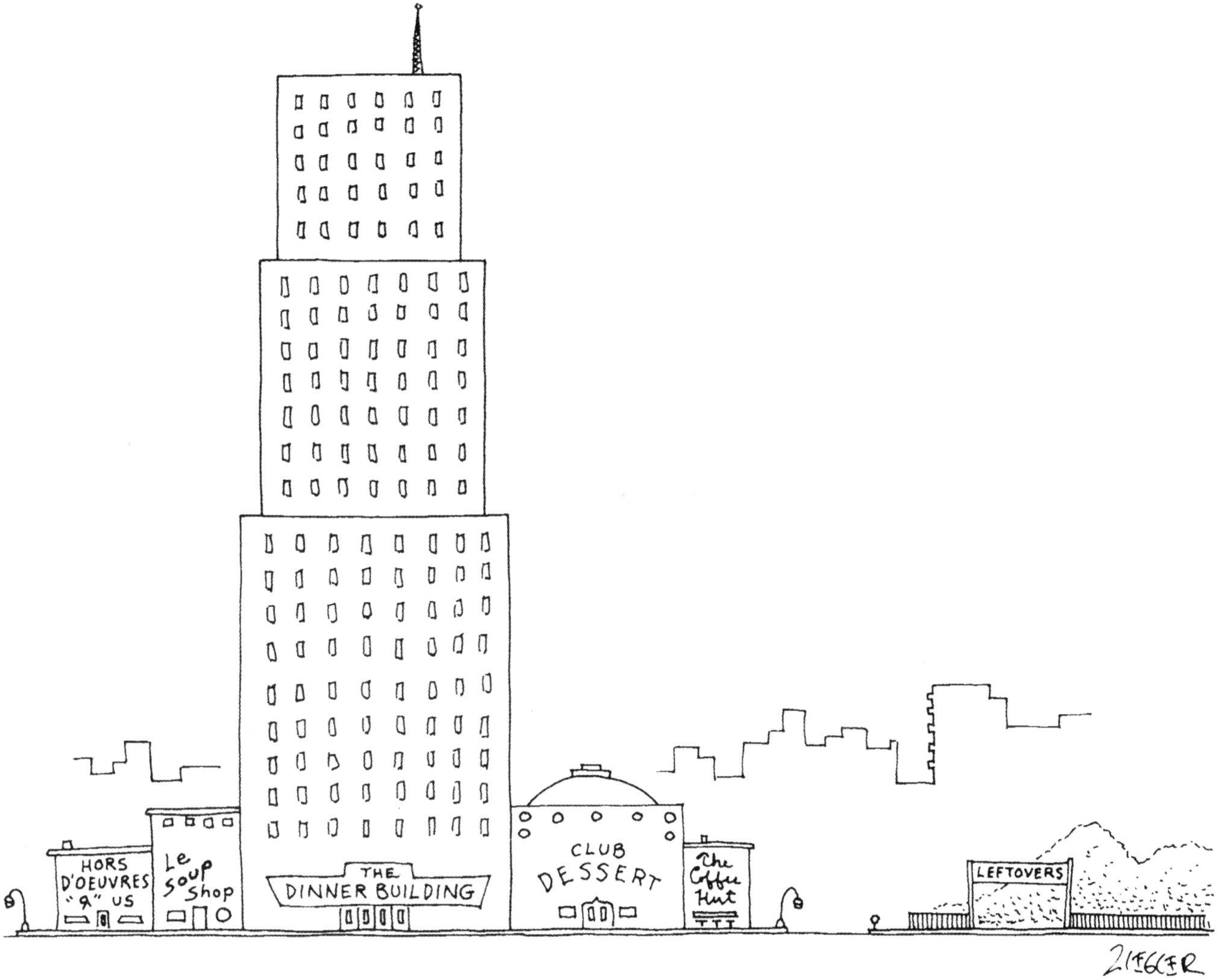
HORS D'OEUVRES "Я" US
Le Soup Shop
THE DINNER BUILDING
CLUB DESSERT
The Coffee Hut
LEFTOVERS
ZIEGLER

"*Let me see if I've got this straight. A rock, a couple of sticks, a leg of mammoth, and some fire.* That's it??"

"*That's the food biz. Celebrity chef one day, graveyard-shift hash jockey the next.*"

"It says: 'My compliments to the chef.'"

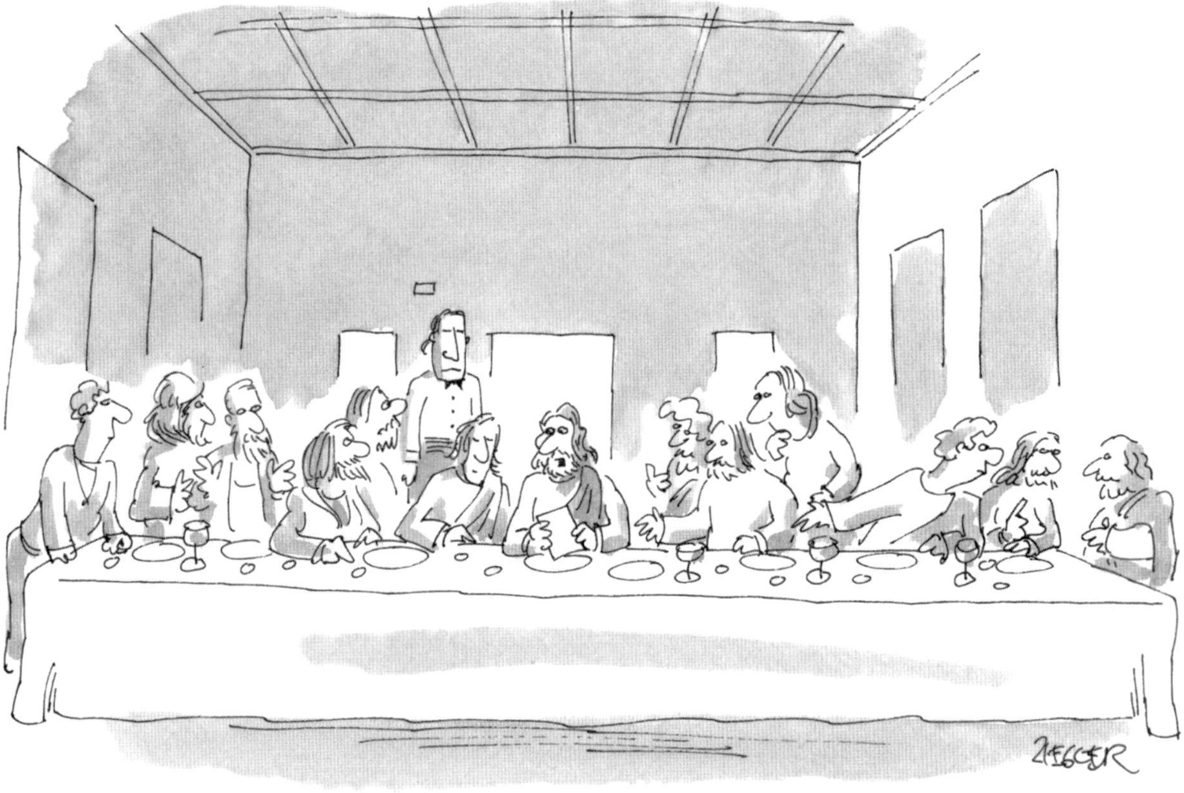
ZIEGLER

"Yikes! Somebody ask him if they take plastic."

"Asparagus."

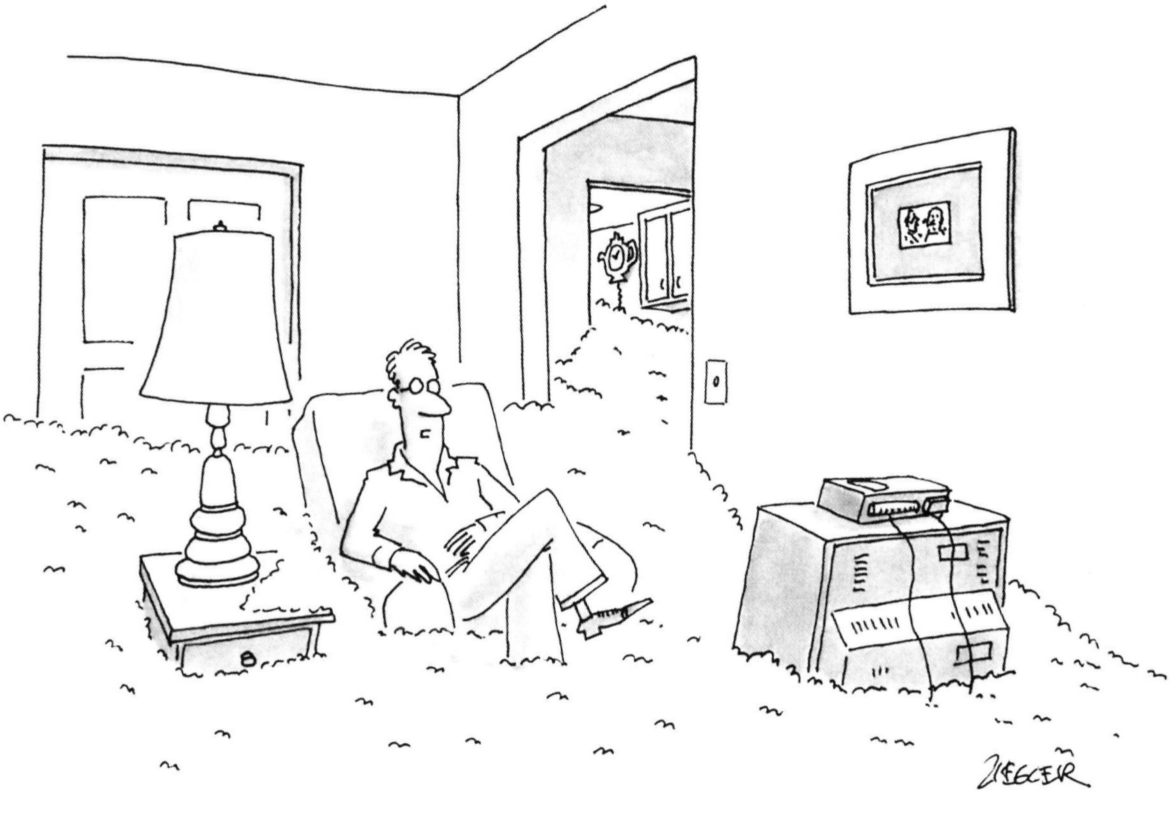
ZIEGLER

"Popcorn's done, honey."

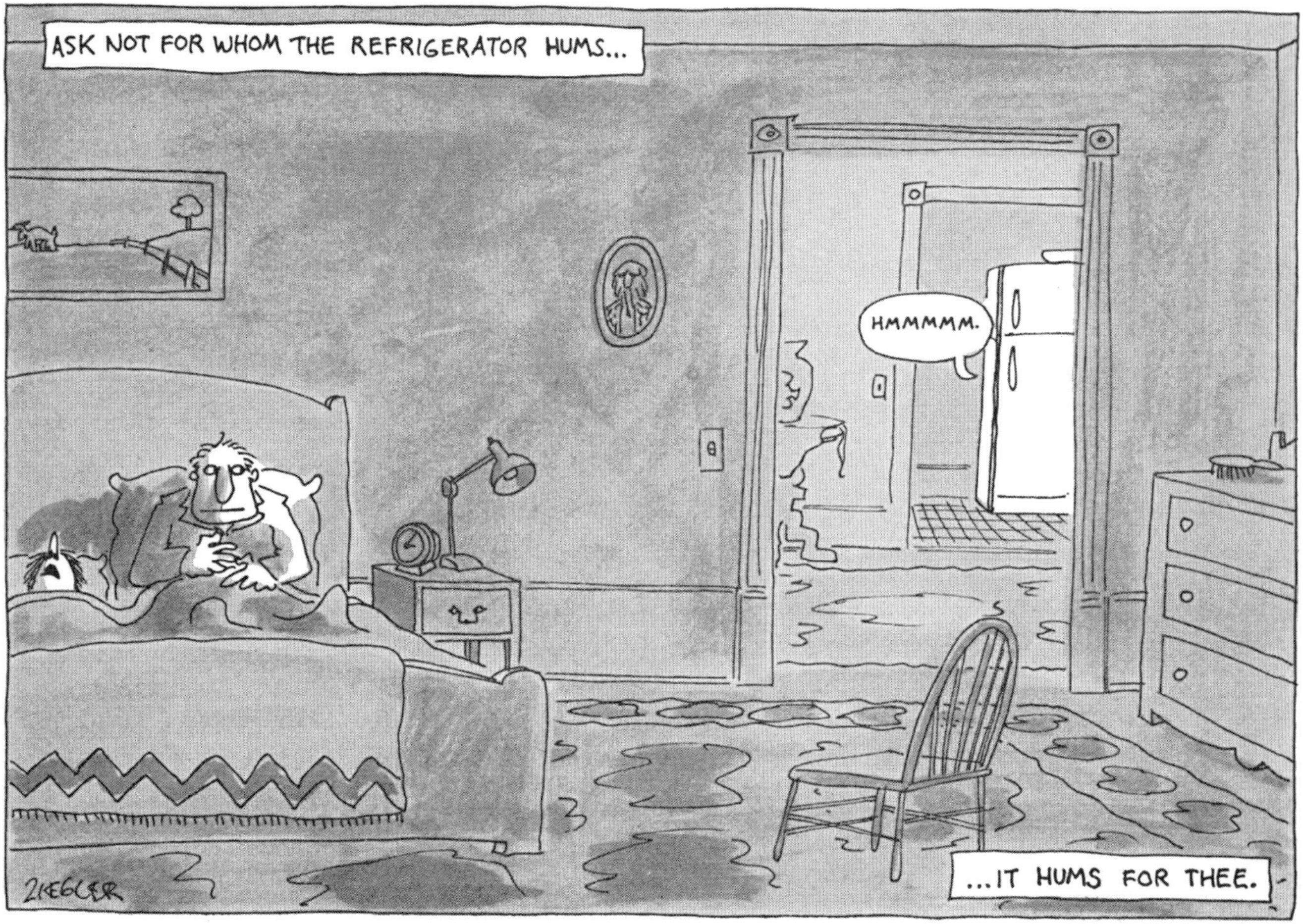
ASK NOT FOR WHOM THE REFRIGERATOR HUMS...
HMMMMM.
...IT HUMS FOR THEE.
ZIEGLER